AS FOR Me anD MY HoUSe2

Also Available

As for Me and My House, Volume 1
50 Easy-to-Use Devotionals for Families

AS FOR ME and MY HOUSE 2

50 Easy-to-Use Devotionals for Preteens and Young Teens

Tom and Lori Ziegler

DPI
DISCIPLESHIP
PUBLICATIONS
INTERNATIONAL

www.dpibooks.org

As for Me and My House—Volume 2
©2008 by DPI Books
5016 Spedale Court #331
Spring Hill, TN 37174

Printed in the United States of America

ISBN: 1-57782-231-5

contents

InTRODUCTion TO VOLUME 2

TiPS FOR GReat PReTeen anD YOUNG Teen DevOTiOnals

As our children get older, family dynamics have a way of shifting and sometimes becoming uncomfortable or more challenging. As our children grow older, they can also grow more moody, more independent, more opinionated and outspoken. These years are full of amazing joys, but can also be bewildering at times—for both parents and kids! Growing up and maturing is one of the hardest things we go through in life.

Here are some suggestions about having family devotionals with older children.

1. Have fun! Family devotionals should be happy, joyful times to build great memories. They should not be consistently full of correction so that your children want to avoid them.
2. Pray for wisdom as your children get older.
3. Talk as a family about your devotionals, and seek the input of the whole family to make it a great time. Parents, you may have to adjust your "style" for devotionals as your children mature.
4. Use family devotionals to create a "safe haven" for every member of the family. This is a time to practice Ephesians 4:29 to make sure that every member of your family is encouraged and built up.
5. Some of the topics in this book are a bit controversial and may open up some great, but challenging discussions. Parents, be careful to listen well and not "jump" on every comment your children make.
6. Ask your children's opinions on topics before sharing your own. If we think differently than they do, our kids may not feel free to share once we speak up.
7. Let your children pick the topic for family devotional once in a while. Give them this book to go through and to let you know what sounds interesting to them.
8. Let your children take turns leading the family devotional

as they get older. You may learn some very interesting things about how your children think and also about how creative they can be!

9. Leave every devotional on a positive note. Even if the topic is serious, leave your family with a sense of hope and excitement about changing. God is a gracious and forgiving Father, and we must make sure that our children learn not only how serious he is about hating sin, but also how serious he is about forgiveness. God keeps absolutely no record of wrongs!

10. Talk about the theme of the devotional during the following week. We all need daily reminders to help us grow and change and embrace the exciting lessons God wants us to learn.

GROWING LIKE JESUS in WISDOM

Luke 2:41–52

OBJECTIVE

We love the fact that Jesus is not just a good example for adults, but for our children as well. Although Jesus was the Son of God, as a child the Bible describes him as "growing," which is what we all want our children to do! We are going to split this scripture into four different devotionals. These devotionals can be done in a sequence, or you may want to use them when you see particular needs that should be addressed in your family.

ACTIVITY

Start this devotional with a short spelling bee. This reminds us that wisdom and knowledge are closely linked, and the children need knowledge to spell the words. Choose words that are appropriate to the ages and progress of your children. Challenge them a little, but don't discourage them.

After the spelling bee, read Luke 2:41–52. Explain to your family that today you will be learning more about growing in wisdom. What is wisdom? The *Scholastic Children's Dictionary* describes it as "knowledge, experience and good judgment." How do we get knowledge? Every year we spend in school helps us grow in our knowledge. If we make good choices, programs we watch on television can also help us grow in our knowledge. Reading books and talking to each other and learning from each other are other ways.

Being inquisitive and interested are important characteristics to teach our children. Ask your children to tell you some of the best things they have learned so far in school this year. Ask them if there are things they are interested in learning more about. We can facilitate our children's desire to grow in their knowledge in many ways: taking them to museums, finding books in the library that they would like, or using the Internet to research different topics. The possibilities are endless!

Talk about what it means to grow. Do we expect the same things from a two-year-old that we expect from a twelve-year-old? Why not? Do we expect more or less from the twelve-year-old? Why?

Discuss the value of learning things every day both at school and from life. Experience is an important part of growing in wisdom. But the most important part of experience is learning the lesson God wants us to learn. We have stressed this over and over with our children. If we don't learn the lesson, then we often end up repeating the same mistake over and over again.

For example, when we are little, we don't understand that touching a hot stove burner will hurt us badly, but as we get older, we would never do that on purpose because we know the outcome will be painful.

This goes along with having good judgment. Good judgment comes from learning the lesson as we experience different aspects of life. Talk about areas in which it is important to have good judgment. Some examples include not lying, deciding to never smoke cigarettes or try drugs, finishing homework and turning it in every day, and being respectful.

APPLiCation

Share ways you have seen each of your children grow in wisdom. Encourage their progress in areas you know have been difficult for them. This is so important for our children. They thrive on our encouragement, even if they seem embarrassed or indifferent at times.

Share with them ways you have been trying to grow in knowledge or wisdom as well. Growing should not stop just because we are finished with school. If we are interested and curious, it will help our children develop these qualities as well.

Plans, Commitments or Follow-Up

Have each family member share one thing they want to learn more about in the next month, and pick a time to get together to share with each other what each person has learned. Learning something new from the Bible is a great goal.

Another idea is to spend time with someone you would like to learn more about. Jesus had many experiences that taught him many things. Everything we learn relates to God in one way or another, so don't limit the topics your children pick to learn about. You can use anything they choose to also teach something about God.

Scripture Memory or Additional Study

Proverbs 4, especially verse 4

GROWING LIKE JESUS in FAVOR WITH GOD

Luke 2:41–52

OBJECTIVE

We all need to be growing in our relationship with God, and we should consistently help our children to do so as well. We love the idea that Jesus "grew" in favor with God. It is a healthy concept that we can teach our children. While we can do nothing on our own to deserve salvation, we can learn more and more about things that will please God and say thank you to him.

ACTIVITY

Start the devotional with some songs your family loves to sing. We love "Thank you, Lord" and "I want to be like Jesus." Singing is a great way to draw us closer to God and to soften our hearts. See if your children have any songs they want to lead. We cannot overestimate the confidence that our children come to have as they take responsibility to do things like lead songs.

APPLiCatiⱺn

Read the whole passage with your children, or ask them to read it out loud. Focus your discussion on Jesus' time in the temple with the elders. His questions and his answers were amazing to them. He was only twelve at the time, but his connection with God was very deep.

Then at the end of the passage it says that Jesus grew in favor with God. How did that happen? Does it mean that Jesus did things that earned his favor with God? We don't think so because the Bible is clear in other places that we have a relationship with God only through his grace.

At the same time, though, we can grow in favor with God as we learn more and more about the things that please God and as we choose to follow those ways. Jesus wanted to please God. He wanted to know God better. He wanted God to be proud of him. Discuss how we can make God proud of us. Perhaps by reading the Bible and praying more often. Or by being kind to the people around us—especially the people in our families!

It also makes God really happy when we talk to him about situations that come up in our day. Talk to your children about praying throughout their day: before school, before taking a test, and after the test to say thank you, and during soccer practice.

Jesus was aware of God's presence. Discuss how we can be aware of God throughout the day and what it means to walk with God. God wants to be involved with everything in our lives. Talking about this has helped our kids realize that having a relationship with God is not just about church or family devotionals, but about letting God be involved in every part of their lives.

PLaNS, CⱺMMitMeNtS ⱺR FⱺLLⱺW-UP

Have every person in the family share one thing they want to focus on in the next week in order to grow closer to God. Follow up at dinner or before bedtime every day to share how it is going, and encourage one another.

Don't use the time to reprimand, but to help everyone realize that growing in favor with God is a process. For the next week, pray together about this every day as a family.

SCRIPTURE MEMORY OR ADDITIONAL STUDY

1 Peter 2:2–3

GROWING LIKE JESUS in FAVOR WITH MEN

Luke 2:41–52

OBJECTIVE

This is a tricky topic for kids. Jesus grew in favor with men, but not all men. Growing in favor with men did not mean that Jesus was out to be a "people pleaser." Because Jesus was growing in his relationship with God and "in favor with God" he was also becoming the kind of person that was attractive to others.

ACTIVITY

Start this devotional with a conversation about different groups of people your children know at school. Ask them to describe the different groups they know about. For example, at one of our kids' school there are the "populars," the "sports people," the "really smart people," and then there's "just everyone else." The populars wear expensive clothes and everyone knows them. They are always together, and if they get split up they are really uncomfortable, according to our child.

In our discussion it also came up that the populars aren't really nice to each other. You will learn a lot about how your children view their world through this discussion.

Ask if they see themselves in any of the groups. If so, which one? And why? If they don't see themselves in any of the groups, ask why not. Ask how they feel about having different groups or cliques.

Try not to pass any judgments on kids at school during this conversation (that is difficult for us as parents), but keep asking questions to draw out your children's opinions. Ask if it is important to try to fit in and why or why not.

APPLiCation

Read Luke 2:52 and also read John 2:13–25. Compare these 2 passages. In Luke 2:52 the Bible teaches us that Jesus grew in favor with men. But then in John 2 he goes into the temple, overturns tables and makes a lot of people really angry. The passage ends in verse 24 saying that Jesus would not entrust himself to men because he knew all people.

While Jesus grew in favor with men, at the same time he had deep convictions about what was pleasing to God. Jesus never compromised his convictions in order to fit in with the crowd or to make someone like him. Jesus was never afraid to say what was true even to his very best friends. This is a hard teaching for many of us.

Discuss the concept of "a little white lie" and how we often don't want to tell the truth because we don't want to hurt someone or we want to fit in with the crowd. People-pleasers have opinions that shift according to the group they are with at the moment. Jesus was not afraid to have convictions because he was also growing in favor with God as he grew up. He had convictions, but he was also kind and gentle and he was trustworthy. We can grow in favor with men by imitating those qualities in Jesus.

Ask: Are we nice to be around, or are we sarcastic? Are we trustworthy, or do we say we will do something and then later "forget"? Are we honest, or do we cheat or lie to get out of being in trouble? Are we disrespectful to teachers so that our peers will think that we are cool?

In order to grow in favor with men, we can't be worried about what our peers think about us all the time. Being kind, honest and trustworthy are important characteristics to God. Those same characteristics are respected and appreciated by most people we come in contact with.

Plans, Commitments or Follow-up

Ask your children to share one area they want to grow in from your discussion. Again, please don't use family devotionals as times to reprimand, but create a safe place where every family member can share and get the help they need.

Let your children know that you understand how hard it can be to imitate Jesus. Share from your own life either now or when you were their age. Commit to pray for each other every day and share victories that you have with each other.

Scripture Memory or Additional Study

John 15:18–25

GROWING LIKE JESUS in Stature

Luke 2:41–52

OBJECTIVE

Growing in stature includes growing physically and in our confidence. People with a presence are usually strong physically, but also have engaging personalities. These are things we can all grow in, and this devotional focuses on helping our children in these areas.

ACTIVITY

If you have a growth chart that you have used to measure the progress of your children, take time to look at it together and marvel at how much they have grown. Notice that we don't usually grow at the same pace all the time. Sometimes it seems like we haven't grown at all, and then all of a sudden we have a sudden growth spurt and jump several inches in a short time. Our kids love to compare their sizes at the same age, and now that they are getting older, they love to compare their height and weight with Mom and Dad!

APPLiCation

Luke 2 describes Jesus as a boy growing in stature. Talk about what that means. "Stature" isn't a word that commonly gets included in daily conversations. The usual definition means the height that someone attains to or the level of development that someone reaches. Both of our kids are concerned about how tall they will be and desire to outgrow their parents by quite a bit if possible.

While God determines our height, there are things we can do to promote good growth and healthy bodies. We need to eat well to grow well! That means making healthy food choices, something our kids don't always think about. Fruits, vegetables, protein, healthy carbohydrates and some fats are all important for us to eat on a daily basis. Talk with your family about what foods everyone likes best and what they really don't like at all. We all need encouragement to try new things. Someone has said that it takes twenty-one "tries" before you might really start to enjoy the taste of some foods.

Our bodies also need activity to grow strong and healthy. God made our bodies to be active, not to sit all day long. Jesus walked a lot. He also grew up helping his father, Joseph, who was a carpenter. Jesus was physically active and that helped him grow!

Walking is a great family activity. Our family also works out together, though Mom isn't as diligent about it as the other three! The kids love it when Dad spends time lifting weights, jumping rope and running with them. Those times have built great memories as well as helping everyone get and stay fit!

Talking is another great family activity. Teaching our children the art of conversation is another way to help them grow in stature as they mature. Young teens often feel awkward and don't always know what to say. Spend time discussing current events or sporting events that interest your children. Teach them to be interested in other people and to ask questions that encourage others to talk as well. As our children mature, it is important to speak to them in a manner that shows you respect them and their opinions. All of this will help them grow in their confidence as they continue to grow taller and healthier!

Plans, Commitments or Follow-up

Talk about what your family can do together to help everyone get or stay healthy. Even deciding to eat one more piece of fruit or a vegetable a day is a great start. Also choose a physical activity that everyone can enjoy together, and pick a time every week to fit it into your schedule. Take advantage of dinner time and car rides to engage your children in as much meaningful conversation as possible.

Scripture Memory or Additional Study

1 Corinthians 6:19–20

A TOUCH OF KINDNESS

5

Mark 1:41–45

OBJECTIVE

This devotional is intended to teach our children how important kindness is. Jesus was the Son of God, all powerful, King of Kings, but he still cared about helping people and showing them love and kindness.

ACTIVITY

Have each family member describe a powerful person that they know about—maybe a teacher, principal, sports figure or political person. Ask if people in authority are always nice to the people around them. Then ask if people with authority might sometimes expect people to be nice to them. Ask why people don't always treat the people around them with the same kindness and respect that they expect from others.

After that, discuss as a family the kind of authority that Jesus had. Paint a picture with words to help your children understand just how much authority Jesus had. John says that Jesus has all authority in heaven and on earth. He was all-powerful, all-knowing; he was with God when God created the whole universe; he could perform miracles and heal people—that takes a lot of authority!

APPLICation

Now read Mark 1:41–45 together. Ask your children to describe what they remember about this passage. Discuss a series of questions as a family.

1. Did Jesus have to heal this man?
2. Did Jesus have to touch him in order to heal him?
3. Why did Jesus touch the man?
4. Do you think the man was probably surprised when Jesus touched him?

Ask them if they know anything about leprosy. It was a common disease in Jesus' time, and it still is in India today. People stayed away from anyone with leprosy back then, and they still do today. In Jesus' time, anyone who had leprosy had to yell "unclean" as they walked around to keep everyone from getting too close to them.

Discuss how it would feel to never get touched, never get a hug from Mom or Dad, never get a pat on the back, never get a "boo-boo" kissed.

Jesus not only healed the man of leprosy, but he reached out his hand and touched him. Maybe for the first time in a long time the man with leprosy felt the warmth of another person's hand on his. The Bible says that Jesus was filled with compassion. Discuss what compassion is and why it is so important.

Jesus is the Son of God. He is very powerful. Yet he still thought about what this sick man with leprosy needed the most. Yes, Jesus healed the disease, but most importantly, he showed the man love and kindness by touching him.

Discuss how we can show kindness to the people around us. Maybe there are kids at school that have a hard time socially. How can we show kindness to them? How would we feel if we never fit in and people made fun of us?

Think of other situations that your children face and apply this principle of showing kindness and respect to others. If we would all imitate this in Jesus, think how different the world around us would be.

Plans, Commitments or Follow-up

Suggest that during this next week, the whole family pray that God will help them to show kindness to someone who needs it. Then share with the family how God answered that prayer.

Scripture Memory or Additional Study

Proverbs 12:25

6

ARGUING AND DISCORD ARE HURTFUL

Psalm 133:1, James 1:19

OBJECTIVE

One of the biggest challenges in raising godly children is helping them to learn to love one another and get along well together. It takes years of patience, prayer and teaching on the part of us parents. The objective of this devotional is to help children realize what it feels like to see two people you love hurting each other—an insight into how God views our arguing and discord.

ACTIVITY

Simulate an argument between you and your spouse right before you sit down for the devotional (if you are a single parent, invite a good friend of your family to participate). It should last about thirty seconds and be obvious to the kids that you are angry with one another. (Please consider the ages and temperaments of your children when you decide what "angry" things to say to each other as you only want to make a solid impression on them, not traumatize them!)

My husband and I simulated a situation where he was sitting

down with our children for a devotional and I was late in joining them. I responded in an irritated way to his urging me to hurry and be part of the time together. I accused him of not helping me enough around the house so I could have the time to be a part of devotionals. (I was "late" because I was folding laundry that had just come out of the dryer.) He responded that I just needed to be better organized and that devotionals were more important than laundry! (you get the idea...)

APPlication

After your "argument," explain that you were not really fighting. It was just to teach them something important. Reassure them that you really do love each other. Ask them the following questions:

1. How did you feel when you saw Mommy and Daddy arguing? (afraid, sad, confused)
2. What did you hear in our voices? (anger, meanness, irritation)
3. Why did you feel afraid or sad when you saw us arguing? (afraid you are going to get divorced, don't like to you talk to each other like that, etc.)

Explain that we see people not being nice to each other every day. Why did it affect them more to see their parents hurting each other and speaking to each other this way? God loves us very much. How do you think he feels about our way of treating each other and speaking to each other? Why?

Read Psalm 133:1 and choose some of the following questions to discuss:

1. Have you had any fights/arguments with each other over the past few days or weeks? What were they about? Why is it so hard to get along and be loving to each other? James 1:19 tells us it comes from selfishness and jealousy—we think about ourselves first and want things for ourselves, pride—we think we know better than others, and laziness—we don't want to make the effort to put ourselves in our brother's/sister's shoes and understand what they might be feeling.
2. When you think back on these arguments you had, do you

see any of these sins in yourself at those times? I know you probably see them in your sister/brother since it's always easier to see other people's sins before our own. What about your own heart as you think back?

Be patient as your children try to express what they think here. They may still have a hard time identifying their sins in the situation. Calmly guide them to humbly rethink their own reactions, even if they were not the ones who "started it" or if they were provoked. You may say things like "I know your sister talked too long on the phone and made you miss that important phone call you were expecting. She has said she was sorry. Do you think what you said to her is the way you would have liked to be treated if you were in her shoes? Do you think that if you had reacted in a more calm or patient way, this whole thing would not have been blown out of proportion and you would not have ended up throwing her iPod on the floor?...or something to that effect.

PLaNS, COMMITMENTS OR FOLLOW-UP

Wrap up the devotional by having each person commit to think before they react the next time they feel angry. Teach them to count to ten before they speak or even better, to go into another room to pray before they respond. Pray together every day for the next week (or longer) about loving one another and not arguing or having discord in the home.

SCRIPTURE MEMORY OR ADDITIONAL STUDY

Romans 12:12–17

Getting Dressed For School

Colossians 3:12–14

Objective

Starting a new school year is always an exciting time and most kids (girls, at least) really seem to look forward to clothes shopping for the new school year. This devotional helps our kids think about how they act and not just about outward clothing. (This can be adapted for use any time during the year.)

Activity

Have your kids hold a fashion show to show you their favorite new school outfit. If you are doing this devotional at a different time of year, have them model their favorite outfit for you. Make sure to have a "runway" and that they model and pose for you as they have seen people on television do.

After they have modeled their clothes, have everyone sit together and talk about why they chose the outfit that they did. How does the outfit make them feel about themselves? New clothes or favorite outfits usually make us feel happy and confident.

Read Colossians 3:12–14. Isn't that funny. God tells us to clothe ourselves, not with pants and shirts, but with inside things. He assumes we will always put our clothes on, but he wants to remind us to put on the right inside things as well.

APPLication

Discuss each of these: compassion, kindness, humility, gentleness, patience. What does each mean? How can we show compassion, kindness, humility, gentleness and patience at school? With our friends? With our teachers? With new kids at school? With each other?

Why is it hard to remember these things sometimes? What is our natural reaction if someone isn't nice to us or if we sit next to a new person at school or on the bus? Do you ever feel afraid to speak to people you might have seen around school but haven't gotten to know? How do you act in those situations? Or if our teacher corrects us?

As you discuss each characteristic, pull out a sign that you made ahead of time to tape on a piece of clothing that your kids have on. For example, tape "compassion" on a t-shirt, "gentleness" on a pair of jeans, etc.

Remind your children that every day as they get dressed they should also think about putting on the "inside clothing" that God talks about. Also discuss how our favorite clothes can make us feel happy or confident, but God wants our happiness and confidence to come from what is inside us, not from what we wear.

Plans, Commitments or Follow-up

Depending on the ages of your children, you could cut out a t-shirt from a piece of poster board and have everyone label it with the characteristic they feel they need to "dress" with every day. You could also make a collage of the words compassion, kindness, humility, gentleness and patience to post on the door so everyone can see it as they leave for school and work everyday as a reminder.

Scripture Memory or Additional Study

Luke 6:45

GUARD YOUR REPUTATION

Daniel 6:15

OBJECTIVE

The objective of this devotional is to show your children the power of having a great reputation. Daniel was an outstanding representative of God in a very godless country. This devotional is intended for older children who can identify with the temptations Daniel faced.

ACTIVITY

Find an article on the Internet or in the newspaper about a person who has been accused of fraud or some other crime. Unfortunately, there have been several people in the past few years that have faced very serious accusations. (For example: the Enron situation.) Read the article and discuss the implications of the crime on the person, the person's family, the company they represent, etc. Emphasize what this crime did to the person's reputation.

APPLICATION

After reading Daniel 6:15 together, discuss the kind of temptations Daniel might have faced on a daily basis in his job. Then discuss the reputation that he had within the government. Discuss what it means to be trustworthy and what it means to distinguish yourself.

Daniel was an amazing example in a very difficult situation. Every day our children go to school in godless places and face temptations of many kinds. We, as parents, also face difficult things in the places we work. Share with your children some of the temptations you face at work (remember to consider the ages and maturity of your children, but also be real with them. Our kids need to know that we struggle and overcome difficult things so that they will know how to face those kinds of struggles themselves).

Ask your kids what it would take for them to distinguish themselves and to have a reputation like Daniel. For example, discuss how we can distinguish ourselves with our homework and class assignments. The following responses help them stand out as shining examples: never handing in assignments late, completing every assignment neatly and thoroughly, never complaining when the teacher hands out homework and projects. Even if no one comments, they can still know they have been a good example. Teenagers often need help being disciplined about doing homework right after school or between school and activities so that they don't procrastinate and stay up too late. This is a great scripture to help build convictions in this area.

Another area to discuss could be home issues. Who we are at home is really who we are! We can have a reputation of being organized and neat at school, but what about those bedrooms?! Being trustworthy at home means not having to be asked twice to help with dinner, set the table, take out the garbage, do dishes, etc. It also means being true to your word.

Plans, Commitments or Follow-up

For the next week, discuss this passage during dinner or at another time that your family spends together. Have the goal of being trustworthy in handing in all assignments on time, participating in class discussions and being helpful around the house. If your children need lots of help in this, focus on one area at a time so that you don't overwhelm them. Once they have victories in one area, praise them often and move on to conquering something else.

SCRIPTURE MEMORY OR ADDITIONAL STUDY

Colossians 3:17, 1 Timothy 4:16

VACATION WITH HAPPY MONEY

Philippians 4:4

OBJECTIVE

Being on vacation can end up being a challenging time for our children to stay happy and grateful. This is a practical lesson to teach the importance of being happy in all situations.

ACTIVITY

Start this devotional with the song "Thank You, Lord" or another song expressing gratitude. Then read the following scriptures:

Proverbs 15:13—"A happy heart makes the face cheerful."

Proverbs 15:30—"A cheerful look brings joy to the heart."

Philippians 4:4—"Rejoice in the Lord always. I will say it again: Rejoice!"

Philippians 2:14–15—"Do everything without complaining or arguing, so that you may become blameless and pure, children of God without fault in a crooked and depraved generation, in which you shine like stars in the universe."

Discuss the scriptures and ask how important it is to God that we are happy. He talks about being happy a lot, so it must be important to him. Ask what things make us happy and what things can make us unhappy. After a short discussion, have a "Popcorn Prayer." Each person prays for one thing that they are thankful for. Go around the family circle several times as new things "pop" into your minds to pray about.

Application

Most families love to go on family vacations. One family came up with a fun way to maintain a joyful spirit during their time together. In the midst of traveling, being with friends and/or family, abnormal sleeping/eating/daily schedules and the stimulation of vacations activities, they often found that they could get too much of a good thing. Emotions would invariably descend into irritability or a complaining spirit.

They found that having a devotional together about the scriptures listed on the previous page was helpful, and they also implemented the following game to serve as a fun way to remind each other to continue to be loving and cooperative.

Start the vacation with an envelope for each person (parents and children), and in that envelope place twenty nickels. This is "Happy Money." Label each envelope with the name of a family member. Dad or Mom can keep the envelopes all together. When anyone in the family gets a bit cranky, starts complaining or arguing, or is generally hard to get along with, talk about it as a family and remove a nickel from that person's envelope. This procedure applies to Mom and Dad, too.

Near the end of the trip, exchange the nickels in each person's envelope for dollars (that is, you receive one dollar for each nickel in your envelope). This provides some extra spending money for the trip.

Two of the best results of this game are (1) it stops the downward spiral of negativity that can develop even in the middle of a great plan for the family to have fun together, and (2) it gives the children opportunities to point out negative attitudes in Mom and Dad and gives us the opportunity to model humility in our response to them.

Plans, Commitments or Follow-up

Happy Money will likely be a fun family memory for you! To follow up after vacation, from time to time remind the children of Happy Money. Ask them what they learned on the trip while the family played this game. And remind them that they can still let you know if you are not having a joyful spirit!

Scripture Memory or Additional Study

Philippians 4:4

Learning to Be Flexible

Genesis 12:1–9

Objective

Learning to accept changes in our lives is a challenge for most of us. This devotional is designed to help our children learn to adapt and to embrace the changes that occur.

Activity

For younger children: If your children have a transformer toy, this will be a great time to get it out and play with it together. As you play, talk about how much fun it is to make the toy become one thing and then another.

For older children: Play a short game of charades, where everyone in the family takes turns acting out an animal. They will have to be flexible in switching from portraying one animal to portraying another.

Application

Our children do not particularly like it when our schedule changes. One of them in particular has always been very conscious of what time we are supposed to be somewhere, when we are leaving, exactly what time Dad would get home, etc. Helping them relax and accept that life as we know it will constantly change has been one of the challenges of our parenting.

Genesis 12:1–9 is a great passage to show our children that often God will call us to change things in our lives and that we need to be ready and willing just like Abram was. God doesn't always call us to move (though sometimes he does and if your family is in that situation, this will be a great passage to share and discuss).

This is an amazing time in Abram's life. Imagine being seventy-five years old and being asked to move...somewhere. God didn't even tell Abram where he was going! Talk about a big change! Abram really needed to be flexible and willing to do whatever God asked him. The change didn't just affect him, but also his wife and his nephew. They packed up everything they had ever accumulated and set out.

Imagine packing up everything in your home, loading it on a big truck and then just starting to drive...without knowing where you would end up.

After discussing these topics for a few minutes, pick some of the following questions to help your family.

1. How would you feel if you were asked to move somewhere else?
2. What would be the hardest thing about moving?
3. Do you think Abram and Sarai's life was different when they were wandering around looking for the place God wanted them to settle?
4. How do you think their life was different?
5. What could have happened if Abram had felt stubborn and decided he didn't want anything to change in his life? Do you think God could have blessed him the same way then? (Read verse 7 together). God wanted to bless Abram a lot.
6. When is a change in plans hard for you?
7. Do you think God will bless you if you are flexible and willing to go along with the changes?
8. How can our family learn to be more flexible?

Plans, Commitments or Follow-up

One of things we have impressed upon our children over time is that they need to relax and just be kids and let us, as parents, figure out the details of life. It helped a lot when they were younger. As they have gotten older and have to learn how to plan more, it has given them more peace because they have watched us handle situations (mostly) in a calm manner. Just remind them of this fact going forward any time they get anxious about change or schedules.

SCRIPTURE MEMORY OR ADDITIONAL STUDY

Proverbs 16:9

Listen to the Heavens

Psalm 19:1–11

OBJECTIVE

The sky has special significance for our family. Living in Africa for fourteen years was a privilege, and the sunsets and afternoon skies were truly amazing. The combination of colors was spectacular. We often noted what a great artist God is. This devotional helps us to focus on how vast and powerful our God is and how he speaks to us all day and all night from his creation.

ACTIVITY

Get up early to watch a sunrise or watch the sunset together one evening. You can also go to www.nasa.gov together to look at some stunning pictures of the galaxies, or you could check out a book at the library and look through it together.

While you are all looking at the pictures or watching the sunrise or sunset, have someone read Psalm 19:1–6 out loud.

The sky has no words, no speech, no sound (except thunder), yet it speaks constantly of God's power, majesty, knowledge and glory. It says that the skies proclaim the work of God's hands.

Discuss how that can be. Ask how each family member feels when they look up at the sky, at the sunrise, sunset or at photos of the stars and galaxies.

How big does God become to them? How big do they feel? Read verses 7–11 together. The Psalmist jumps straight from the skies proclaiming God's glory to the words, laws and statutes of the Bible. The first focus is on God's creation and the second on his word.

God knows we need visual aids to help us understand him more, and so he surrounds us with an amazing sky to speak to us every day about his greatness, his vastness, his everlasting power.

The sun never stops rising and setting. God keeps the sun and earth on their path constantly so that "nothing is deprived of its warmth."

If God cares enough to surround us with examples like that, we can trust him to also give us laws, decrees and statutes that will guide and direct our lives in the right path.

APPLicatiON

Verse 11 tells us that there is great reward in keeping (obeying) God's laws. Discuss ways as a family that this has been true for you. We often share with our children how thankful we are that we had an opportunity to study the Bible and change the direction of our lives. If that had not happened we wouldn't have met and gotten married, and we wouldn't have had the amazing experiences in Africa or the wonderful family that we have.

We also share with them the challenging times we experienced when we moved to Africa, how difficult it was to adapt to a new culture and way of life.

Following God's ways doesn't mean everything will be perfect or easy, but the outcome is always good.

Moving back to the United States was difficult as well, but we have seen God bless us in many ways, and we have all learned some great lessons along the way.

Share examples from your own lives and experiences, and ask your children if they have seen the same principles at work in their lives. Ask everyone to share one thing that has been difficult for them to trust God in lately. How does this devotional (and these scriptures) help put that in perspective?

Plans, Commitments or Follow-Up

Write down the challenge that each family member shared. Ask everyone to commit to pray for each other during the week and for however long it takes to overcome that issue. Pray together as a family as well. Don't forget to ask each other as the weeks go by how they are doing in learning to trust in this area.

Scripture Memory or Additional Study

Psalm 24:1

NO WORLDLY POINT OF VIEW

2 Corinthians 5:11–16

OBJECTIVE

This scripture is making special reference to our having a ministry of reconciliation. However, another principle comes out of it that can help our children to have and keep the right spiritual perspective about themselves and others (see verse 16). In magazines, on television, billboards and other forms of advertising we are inundated with worldly images of what is "in" and "cool" and "right." These have damaging consequences on how we view ourselves and others. This devotional will help put the world in its proper perspective.

ACTIVITY

Get several magazines and look through them as a family. Notice how thin all the models are and how many of the articles focus on outward appearances and not on character traits.

Discuss ads you have seen (or in our case, have flipped past as quickly as possible) that use sensuality or women's scantily dressed bodies to sell everything from clothes to cars.

Be sensitive to the ages of your children and the struggles they may be facing personally, but this is a topic that we need to address as families to take away Satan's power.

Read 2 Corinthians 5:11–16. Compare what you read in this passage with what you have seen in magazines and on television. In the media, the important message is often what someone looks like. Advertisers use attractive men and women to help sell the idea that if you use a certain product you can have the life that these people have.

Verse 16 of this passage says that because of what we understand about God from the preceding verses, we will regard no one from a worldly point of view any more.

Over and over in the Scriptures, God points us to look at our hearts, at the inside, at our character and actions, but the world keeps pointing us to what we look like, how we dress, and what cool products we have. The world keeps trying to tell us and our children that "we *are* what we have and wear" while God wants us to focus on who we are as people and how we treat one another. These are the most important things in life.

APPLication

Use this discussion to focus on some of the following questions. Choose questions you think will help your family the most.

1. When you keep seeing these ads and articles, how does it affect the way that you look at yourself? Do you ever feel critical of your appearance and think you should be taller, thinner, stronger, etc.?
2. How does the world's point of view differ from what God desires from us?
3. When other people have "cool" products (TVs, clothing, iPods, etc.) and you don't, how does that make you feel?
4. Is it wrong to have those items? (No, but God doesn't want us to think those things are what makes us acceptable or valued.)
5. When you look in the mirror, do you see how wonderful you are, or do you see everything that needs to change?
6. How can we change the way we look at our appearance? (God made each of us special and unique in our character. We are wonderfully made according to Psalm 139:14.)

Plans, Commitments or Follow-up

Share the wonderful things you love about each member of your family, and allow everyone else the time to do the same. Give everyone a note card and have them write down the three best things about themselves that they will focus on in the next week. Focus on the things of the heart rather than outward appearances.

Scripture Memory or Additional Study

Psalm 139:13–14

WHY SO MANY RULES?

Deuteronomy 7:11–15, 8:1

OBJECTIVE

This devotional is designed to help our children understand that the commands and laws God gave to the Israelites were there to bless them so that they would stay healthy. Then God could give them the land he had promised them. God loved his children and wanted them to enjoy his blessings and not get sick. He gave them rules to protect them from disease and sickness. The Egyptians and other people who did not have God's rules or did not obey them, did not know some of the things that made them sick or made them die.

ACTIVITY

Have everyone in the family line up in front of the sink and wash their hands with soap and water. After everyone has finished washing their hands, sit down around the table and ask your children if they know why they wash their hands. Ask them if it is just to get the dirt off or if there is another reason they are asked to wash their hands. Ask them if they enjoy washing their hands. Ask them when it is especially important for them to wash their hands.

Read Numbers 19:16–22.

Ask your children what God asked the Israelites to do here. Why did God want them to wash so much? Explain that God loved his people and wanted them to stay healthy.

Explain that you love your children and want to keep them healthy as well.

Explain to your children that men only discovered bacteria and germs just over 100 years ago. Thousands of years before bacteria and germs were discovered by men God knew they were there. God knew that the Israelites needed to wash the germs away to keep from getting sick.

Explain that some germs and bacteria can make us very sick. God wanted the Israelites to wash very well so that they would wash the bacteria away that they got from touching things that were unclean.

APPLication

Today we can get sick from germs and bacteria as well. We get colds and flu and sometimes more serious sicknesses from bacteria. The best thing we can do to help us not to get sick is wash our hands frequently during the day. Especially before we eat, after we go to the bathroom, play outside or touch animals.

In hospitals there are many germs. Doctors and nurses have to wash their hands a lot to keep from passing germs from one sick person to another. Here is a sign found in hospitals today to remind doctors, nurses and other health professionals to wash their hands frequently:

5 steps to clean Hands

1. Use soap and running water.
2. Rub your hands vigorously for 10 to 15 seconds.
3. Wash all surfaces: back of hands, wrists, between fingers under nails.
4. Rinse well.
5. Dry hands with a disposable paper towel.

(Information from the Department of Human Services Communicable Disease Control Branch)

People who work in restaurants have to obey these rules as well so that they don't pass germs on to their customers.

Sometimes it is hard to follow the rules. Back when God gave rules to his people, they did not know the reason behind them. They only knew that God loved them and wanted what was best for them.

Today we know why God gave some of these commands because we have learned about things that can make us sick.

We may not always understand the reason why our mothers and fathers give us rules to obey. We need to know that our parents love us and want what is best for us. Maybe one day we will understand a lot more. For now we just need to obey.

PLans, Commitments or Follow-up

Ask your children which household rule is the hardest for them to obey. Ask if they know why it is a rule. Explain the reason behind each rule they bring up. When our children are small (two–four years old) they need to learn to obey just because we are the parents and they need to listen, but as they get older it helps them if we sometimes explain how we think and why something is important to us.

Scripture Memory or Additional Study

Colossians 3:20

WHat's on YOUR MinD?

Philippians 4:8

OBJectiVe

Our mind is a powerful tool, one that we don't always use in a positive manner. It is important to teach our children the value of being aware of their thoughts. We also need to give them the vision of having the power to control their thoughts and dwelling on topics that will add value and significance to their lives. This devotional helps each family member to identify negative thoughts and learn how to turn them around to become positive and helpful.

ACtiVitY

Begin the devotional by playing a word association game. When a parent says a word, everyone shares the first thing that comes to mind. Parents, be creative with this. Think of words that will push buttons with your children both positively and negatively. For example: homework, vacation, Christmas, chores, sports, crafts, etc. Note how some subjects make one person react positively and another negatively.

APPLiCatien

Read Philippians 4:8 together. Discuss the game you just

As For Me and My House

played and how quickly each person's thoughts changed as Mom or Dad brought up different subjects. Ask how that same thing happens to us as we go about our days.

For example, what happens when your children are at school in class and someone answers a question incorrectly? What is their first thought? Is it positive and helpful, or do they look down on the person for being "stupid" or not paying attention. What if they are the one who answers the question wrong? What thoughts run through their minds then?

Parents, share times that you have thought negatively either about yourself or about someone at work, in traffic, etc. Or share about a time that someone hurt you and instead of talking about it, you stewed over things in your mind and just got angry.

Talk about how it makes you feel to walk around with all the negative thoughts going through your mind.

Look back at Philippians 4:8 and talk about the things God wants us to think about (true, noble, right, pure, lovely, admirable, excellent, praiseworthy). Get a piece of paper and make a list together as a family of ten "true" things to think about over the next week. For example, it is true that God loves us. It is also true we are fearfully and wonderfully made, so we are special.

Then make a list of ten things that are "noble." It is noble to stick up for someone who is being picked on at school. It is also noble and right to be nice and kind to each other at home.

Go through the scripture and make a list of ten items for each good thing that God wants us to focus on in our daily thoughts. Maybe you won't be able to think of ten things all at once, but that's okay.

Plans, Commitments or Follow-up

Post your family's lists on the refrigerator or other family notice board so that everyone can see them on a daily basis. Talk about them during the week, and add to any list that you can every day.

Praise each other for thinking of new ways to apply this scripture during the day. And talk about it every night at dinner to see how studying this together is helping your family.

48

SCRIPTURE MEMORY OR ADDITIONAL STUDY

2 Corinthians 10:5

MUSIC TO GOD'S EARS

Psalm 149:1–5

OBJECTIVE

Praising God through music brings joy to our hearts and often peace to our weary minds and bodies. Listening to music can be soothing, uplifting, invigorating and just plain fun. David sang and danced in praise to God. The Bible teaches us to sing songs and hymns to God with gratitude in our hearts (Colossians 3:16). This devotional is simple in form, but will impact your family in amazing ways.

ACTIVITY

Depending on how musical your family is, you can approach this devotional several ways. If members of your family play instruments, ask them in advance if they could prepare and play a song or two for the devotional this week. If anyone sings exceptionally well, ask them to prepare a special solo or duet to perform. If your family loves music, but are not especially gifted, pick out some special CDs to listen to together.

APPLICATION

Read Psalm 149:1–5 together and explain that today for our devotional we are simply going to sing together and praise God through our music. God loves it when we sing, no matter how out of tune we may be. He gave us our voices and appreciates all our efforts to praise him.

If your family has a special set of songs you love to listen to, put the music on and sing along. Or you can get out a song book and pick several family favorites to sing together. Ask your children to lead some of their favorite songs as well.

After you spend time singing together, have a special prayer and thank God for all of the blessings in your lives. We find that singing together opens our hearts and shows our family just how good God is and how much he has blessed our lives.

After the prayer, spend a few minutes sharing how singing makes you feel.

Plans, Commitments or Follow Up

Before dinner every night for the next week, include a song either before your prayer or at the end of the meal. Consider how singing together can change the atmosphere at the end of a hectic day.

Scripture Memory or Additional Study

Psalm 146:1–2

16

WHATEVER YOU DO

Colossians 3:23

OBJECTIVE

The goal of this devotional is to help your children realize that following Jesus is not just about going to church and reading the Bible, but about applying the principles in the Bible to our everyday lives. The idea from Colossians 3:23 is that "whatever" we do applies to school work, homework, sporting activities, musical instruments, dance, drama, helping around the house, making our beds, keeping our rooms clean...you get the picture!

ACTIVITY

There are several possibilities for this one. Choose whichever fits best for your family. One activity is to find a copy of a math, spelling or grammar worksheet and have everyone in the family fill it out. You can find books of worksheets, or you can get one off the Internet. The kids may wonder why they are doing school work for family devotional, but encourage them to work on the paper, and tell them you will explain later.

Another idea is to have everyone sit down to dinner, but not have the table set at all. Then have Mom or Dad bring in a couple of cans of cold spaghetti or other prepared food and just set it on the table. One or more of the kids will probably question why the table isn't set and wonder how we are supposed to eat cold, canned food. Respond that you were just too busy and did not really feel like cooking anything, so you figured this would be okay. Then have a can opener to begin opening "dinner," and ask someone to go get plates, forks, etc.

When you serve your family their real dinner, tell them that you will explain about the previous "dinner plan" during your devotional time.

Application

Read Colossians 3:23 with your family, and ask them how they think it may apply to whichever activity you chose to begin with. Explain that Colossians 3:23 is an important teaching from the Bible because in one verse God tells us how important it is to give our very best effort to whatever we do in our lives every day.

Ask for examples of what it means to work at something with all your heart. Talk about how they feel about doing their school work and if they give their very best effort in class every day. Or with their homework—do they work hard to finish it up, or do you as parents have to push them?

Talk about what God expects. (An important note in this is that God never says we have to be "the best" at anything. He only asks that we give our very "best effort" at everything. There is a big difference in the two, and it is important to help our children understand what God and we as parents expect of them. Pushing our children to be the best is very far from this teaching and can damage them in many ways.)

If you chose to go with the second idea, ask your children how it made them feel when you told them you didn't feel like getting them anything more to eat and that you were busy.

Ask them how they think it makes God feel when we don't give our best effort at whatever we do. This is a great time to talk about household chores, homework, or any other area where you have seen your children give only partial effort. Have every person in the family share one thing they have not been giving their best at and share how they plan to change it during the next week.

Plans, Commitments or Follow Up

Follow up at dinner every night and encourage the changes you see in each other.

This scripture applies to our character, and changing things in our character often takes work and patience. We use this scripture often in our home to encourage each other and to remind each other what God expects in our lives. This devotional can be a reminder or wake up call, but we need to instill character in a loving way over time with our children.

Scripture Memory or Additional Study

Matthew 25:21

17

You can't Hide From God

Judges 6:1–16

OBJECTIVE

Whenever things aren't going well in our lives, it is easy to try to hide from God and others, and it is also easy to blame God for our problems. We can forget that things that happen are often consequences of mistakes we have made along the way. This devotional helps us see that God is aware of our every move and that he has a plan to help us fix things if we will just turn to him, ask for help, and then obey him.

ACTIVITY

Gather your family together in one room. Then have one parent go into another room and begin reading Judges 6:1–16. Let it be loud enough to hear, but just barely. After reading several verses, come back into the room and ask your kids why they think you left to read. Did it make them feel close as a family? Did it make it easy to understand what God had to say?

Discuss how sometimes when we do something wrong, we can feel like we are hearing God's word from a distance, that it is hard to connect with each other and with God when we are trying to hide something.

Read the rest of the passage to the family.

APPLiCaTiON

The Israelites had been disobedient to God, and so God had allowed the Israelites to suffer the consequences of their behavior. He allowed the Midianites to teach them a lesson. When things got really hard, they blamed God for their situation. Was it God's fault that the Midianites had taken over? Gideon told the prophet that God had abandoned them. Was that true? Who was the one who turned away in the first place, Israel or God? Have you ever blamed God when you have to suffer a consequence of your own actions?

When the angel of the Lord came to find Gideon, where was Gideon? Why was he in the winepress? He was scared and acting cowardly. How can we be like him sometimes? Have you ever tried to "hide" when things weren't going well?

Sometimes we stop praying or stop reading our Bibles because we feel guilty about something we have done, or sometimes we stop because we feel like God doesn't care and isn't listening to us.

Had God forgotten the Israelites? No. Will he forget about us even if we are disobedient and turn away from him? No. Will God let us go through difficult times in order to help us learn a lesson? Yes. Does that mean that God doesn't love us? Actually, letting us learn our lessons is one of the best ways for God to show us his love.

When the time is right, God also always provides a way for us to turn back and experience great victories, just like he did in this passage with Gideon. God's plan for victory was not what Gideon expected and his plan for us isn't always what we expect either.

God told Gideon to go in the strength he had and that is also what God expects of us. When we have been hiding away, we don't always feel like we have the strength we need to change or grow. God helped Gideon, though, and he will also help us and give us whatever we need in order to grow and be different.

Plans, Commitments or Follow Up

Have each family member share one way they have felt weak and felt God's discipline. Help each other make a plan to change and be different in the next week. Remember to pray for each other every day.

Scripture Memory or Additional Study

Matthew 28:20

can You count the stars?

Genesis 15:5, Isaiah 40:26

OBJECTIVE

These passages help us to understand how big and powerful God is, but also that he is interested in each of us individually.

ACTIVITY

At a park, a campsite or even in your backyard, have a cookout, and then put a blanket down on the ground. Have everyone lie down and look at the stars. It is always so stunning to see how bright the stars are when we get away from the city lights! Talk about these two passages.

Tell the kids to try to count the stars. Talk about how big God is and how powerful he is. He calls the stars out every night and knows each one by name.

Tell them that though there are millions of children who live in the world, God knows each of them by name. Talk about how special every child is to God and how he is concerned about everything in their lives as well.

APPLication

Sometimes it is hard for children to connect and understand that God really cares about each and every person. It helps them to know that if God cares enough to call the stars out by name and there are so many of them, then it makes sense that God can know each and every child by name as well.

PLans, Commitments or Follow Up

Sometimes the best follow up to a family devotional time is just the special memory that everyone holds in their hearts. When things get hectic, you can always remind each other of the peace you all experienced as you lay there and looked up at God's heavens. And remind each other that even when life is busy, we can still have that same peace because God is always with us and calls us by name.

SCRipture Memory or Additional Study

Isaiah 40:11

CHOOSING YOUR FRIENDS WISELY

1 Corinthians 15:33

OBJECTIVE

The objective of this devotional is to take the time to think more deeply about the friends we choose to hang out with. Our friendships influence us in many ways and often determine the direction we take during various times in our lives. We need to think about who we share our secrets with and who we spend the most time with. What implications are there to our lives if we choose our friends wisely? What if we don't choose so well? During this devotional we will share some ways that our friends affect us (good *and* bad examples).

ACTIVITY

Have everyone search out verses in the book of Proverbs to find characteristics that can either *help* or *hurt* our relationships. Take turns reading out loud the scriptures you find. A few examples are Proverbs 10:18, 10:23, 12:16, 12:22, 12:26, 15:4, 15:30, 16:20–21, 18:2, 27:9. There are many more.

Discuss the meaning of each of the proverbs. Parents, remember that while the wording may seem straightforward to you, sometimes the Proverbs are confusing to our children and need explanation depending on their life experiences.

APPLication

Discuss how important it is to choose our friends wisely as we grow older. (Parents have to do this as much as the children!) When our children are young, often as parents, we choose who they will be friends with. We decide who they will hang out with and have play dates with.

As our children grow older and become more independent, they make those decisions for themselves. While Jesus was kind and friendly to everyone, he carefully chose the men that he spent the most time with.

Read 1 Corinthians 15:33 as a family. Ask everyone to think of the friends that they are closest to at church, school, work or in the neighborhood. Then have everyone ask themselves, "Does my friend help me to be closer to God or take me further away from him?" This may not be the appropriate time to discuss specific relationships, but more a time to give your family the chance to think about the direction their friendships are taking them. We would suggest that talks about specific friends (negative influences especially) be relegated to a private talk at a later time.

Use this time to discuss the importance of being a good influence in friendships as well. Not only do we need to think about how others affect us, but also what kind of company we are in the friendship as well. Discuss what helps you to be more godly. What kinds of influences are important in your life to help you become the person that God planned for you to be?

Plans, Commitments or Follow Up

Make a list of characteristics that help friendships to be positive (encouragement, laughter, care and concern about each other, similar interests, sharing positive experiences, genuine happiness about your friend's successes, etc.).

Make another list of characteristics that can hurt friendships (gossip, "dissing" each other or the people around you, competitiveness, selfishness, being bossy, etc.).

Pray together as a family to be great friends to those around you and also that God will lead you and give you wisdom to choose your friends wisely.

SCRIPTURE MEMORY OR ADDITIONAL STUDY

Proverbs 18:24

CHURCH PiZZa

1 Corinthians 12:12–20

OBjECTiVE

This devotional demonstrates how God cares about us and carefully arranges every one of us "just as he wanted." It is designed to help us realize how God sees equality between the members of the Body of Christ and how each member's role is important, special and unique to the church.

ACTiViTY

Everyone will make their own individual pizza.

Ingredients. Pizza dough (make this yourself or purchase it), roller pin, pizza stone or pan, pizza cutter, pizza sauce, and toppings of your choice: tomatoes, olive oil (put on crust before baking), bacon , cheese, onions, mushroom, pepperoni, hamburger meat, pineapple chunks, garlic, pesto, or whatever else you like.

Setting: Play music; set a fun atmosphere. Discuss making the pizza and how to make the crust (work to knead dough and flatten it out). Talk about each of the ingredients, how they are all individually unique, how God made each one for us, but when placed all together they make a pizza.

Cover the pizza with cheese and sauce. Emphasize the placement of these ingredients. For example, it doesn't work well to put the shell on top of ingredients, etc. While each person may choose different toppings, it is not the individual ingredients that make a pizza a pizza, but the combining of all of them together.

Bake for approx 10–12 minutes or until done (times may vary) at 425 degrees F. As you put the pizza in the oven, take one or two items off the pie and let them fall to the bottom of the oven. (Caution: be careful not to cause a fire!)

APPLication

1. While eating the pizza open the scriptures and discuss 1 Corinthians12:12–21
2. Questions:
   a. Is a mushroom or one ingredient by itself a pizza? Obviously not. In the same way, no one person makes up the church. We need each other and together we form the Body of Christ. When the ingredients are placed together in the heat they become very closely related—one. A change occurs with baking. We need to be closely related and united as one.
   b. Which ingredient is the best? None. Every one is different, adding unique flavors to the pizza. Together they equally make a great tasting pizza. Together the disciples of the church make a great and complete body to give praise to God. Each one is vitally and specifically important. And no one is more important than anyone else.
   c. What is the foundation of the pizza? The crust as the foundation holds together all the parts. In the church we build our spiritual foundation on the word of God the Scriptures. It is the Bible that holds all the disciples together and unified.
   d. What is Christ's role in the church? Explain that the sauce represents the blood of Jesus (tactfully). How it covers over the church to present it radiantly to God without stain wrinkle or blemish. Jesus arranges it, he took away its sins, and he leads and loves it.
   e. Was it easy to make the pizza and did it just appear? It takes energy, time and work to build a pizza/church. It takes time to build it (build relationships/spread and study the Word), buy ingredients (sacrificial giving), cut

up ingredients (organization), etc. But it is a joyful experience. (You will see it is a blast making the pizza.)

f. What happens when you leave the protection and comfort of God's Family? Take the burnt and nasty remnant from the oven, and illustrate the symbol of our lives when we leave the protection of the Body of Christ. (Make this point in light heartedness with a mixture of seriousness! Let them answer.)

Plans, Commitments or Follow Up

The church should be the center of life and our means of existence. It is where we grow and become encouraged and strengthened. Discuss as a family how everyone can be a more involved part of God's church. Think of other families you can reach out to in order to build closer relationships. Discuss how special it is that God created his church for us to be a part of. Ask each family member to share something they love about church and how they feel being a part of it.

Scripture Memory or Additional Study

1 Corinthians 12:18
Romans 12:3–5

THE LOST COIN

Luke 15:8–10

OBJECTIVE

It's great to find something valuable that has been lost. God rejoices when we stop trying to hide from him and let ourselves be "found" by him. This devotional can help our kids understand how excited God gets about someone deciding to follow him.

ACTIVITY

Hide something valuable in the main room of your home. Pick something special that your children will highly value (toys, candy, trading cards, etc.—make it age appropriate). Tell the children what has been "lost." Ask them to try to find it (make it a slight challenge to find the item). You can equip them with flashlights to better dramatize the search.

APPLICATION

Read the passage and pick out some questions from the following list to help your family grasp the concept from this passage that God has a deep desire to have a close relationship with us. How many questions you choose and how long the discussion goes will depend on the ages of your children.

- Why isn't the woman satisfied with the nine other coins?
- What steps does she take to find the lost one?
- How long will she look for it?
- Whom does she represent in this story? Whom does the coin represent?
- How long will God search for you?
- What steps will he take to find you?
- What does the woman do after she finds the coin? Why?
- How much does she care about the coin?
- How much does God care about you?
- How does a sinner repent? Can you think of a sin you've committed? How can you repent?
- What does God do after you return (i.e. repent) to him?
- How can we give God a reason to throw a party today?

Plans, Commitments or Follow Up

End the devotional with a party, sharing your family's favorite dessert and dancing to illustrate the party in heaven that God throws when one person repents. Ask each family member how this devotional changes the way they think about repentance and how they feel knowing that God will keep searching for them at all costs, hoping to find that "lost coin."

Scripture Memory or Additional Study

Luke 15:10

FEAR NO ONE!

1 Samuel 15:24–28

OBJECTIVE

Fear of what other people think of us is one of Satan's greatest tools, used to take and keep our eyes off God. Fear can cause us to stop trusting God and his word. In this devotional, we look at a great man's moment of weakness and explore the consequences. Saul's fear of the people caused him to sin and lose his place as king over Israel. Our fear of people also can cause us to sin.

ACTIVITY

Simulate the school lunch room at your dining room table. Have each child take a turn playing himself or herself at school in each scenario. Everyone else in the family plays the lunch crowd of kids. Set up a different temptation/intimidation for each child. Following are some ideas—if they don't fit your children, consider others that might work better.

- Temptation scenario 1: open your lunch bags and get ready to eat; stare right at the first volunteer (the family member who is playing self at school). Attempt to simply use your stares to frighten him/her from praying before eating. Then make fun of them when they do pray.
- Temptation Scenario 2: Have one from the crowd Say he/she is going to tell a dirty joke. Everyone says, "Yes, go ahead and tell it." But how does the family member playing self respond?

- Temptation Scenario 3: All begin to gossip about one of the kids who is not sitting at the table.
- Temptation Scenario 4: All begin to grumble and complain about the unfairness of your teacher.

After you've completed a scenario for each child, discuss how fear of people became a real temptation to compromise our beliefs and even sin against God. Then discuss how they can remember to choose faith over fear each time they face a crowd.

APPLication

Read I Samuel 15:24–28 as a family and choose some of the following questions to discuss the role fear played in causing Saul to compromise and ultimately to disobey God.

- Why does Saul sin?
- Is it good that he recognizes why he sins?
- Whose voice did Saul obey?
- What would Saul have done if he were faced with your lunchroom crowd?
- Why is it dangerous to reject the word of God?
- How would the story be different if Saul had obeyed God instead of letting the people intimidate him?
- What are situations you face that cause you to fear what others think of you? Parents, be sure to share temptations you face at work or with your neighbors (and that you had as a kid, if you can remember). It is helpful to share both victories and disappointments as well to help your children learn how grow and change.

Plans, Commitments or Follow Up

Pray together as a family to be confident in God and to have deep convictions about living and acting in ways that please Him. Commit to praying for each other during the week. Use family dinner times to share temptations and victories in this area of your life.

Scripture Memory or Additional Study
1 Samuel 15:24

23

WHERE DO YOU FIT?

1 Corinthians 12:14–20

OBJECTIVE

This scripture teaches us that God created each person for a special purpose. In our culture, however, it is fashionable to blend in with the crowd and imitate what is seen and heard in movies and on television and adopt these attitudes as part of our character. Our children can learn from this study that God created them to be originals, not copies, so that they would fill a purpose in this life that only they can fill.

ACTIVITY

Give each person an identical small jigsaw puzzle (not more than twenty-five pieces).

Prior to the devotional, switch one piece from each puzzle so that when they are assembled, there will be a duplicate (or two, depending upon how many puzzles you have) in each making it impossible to complete.

When your children assemble the puzzle, notice the looks on their faces when they try to fit pieces in that don't fit or when they figure out that they have a duplicate. Encourage them to try to make it fit and note their reactions.

Application

Read 1 Corinthians 12:14–20. Discuss what it means to be different and set apart for God's purpose and why it is important to be ourselves and not to be like others. You can also discuss what happened when they tried to fit the duplicate into the empty space. It wouldn't go because it was not created for that spot; the ear cannot be the eye (verse 16).

Share verses 17 and 18 with your children again. Emphasize that God has designed us perfectly and arranged our places in life. By trying to imitate someone else, we forfeit our originality and we miss out on something wonderful God has planned just for us.

Make sure to emphasize that God wants us to play a role in building up his church. We can't play someone else's role, but we can play whatever role God gives us.

Here are some questions to ponder and discuss together:

1. How does it make you feel to know that God created you for a special purpose?
2. Is it wrong to imitate someone? Why or why not?
3. When you tried to make the piece fit, what happened? What can you learn from this?

How much are you yourself, and how much do you try to be like someone else (i.e. hair styles, clothes, music tastes, choice of expressions or words)?

Plans, Commitments or Follow Up

Ponder God's purpose for your lives. You could start by identifying the gifts and talents that God has given you and asking your children to do the same. Help them if they get stuck or if they can't identify their talents accurately. Then ask how those talents can set them apart for God's purpose? Make a note of their answers. You can use these as a starting point for developing your children's gifts for God.

Scripture Memory or Additional Study

Ephesians 2:10

24

Make Your Own Memories

Judges 6

OBjective

As our children are getting older, part of their "job" is to become more mature and more independent. Our job is to equip them to be independent and get them ready to lead successful, productive lives. This devotional will help you introduce the idea that as your children grow up, they will be building their own lives, their own memories, and their own relationship with God. Growing can be scary, but Gideon shows us that God has a plan and is right there with us to help along the way. (Although devotional number 17 is also about Gideon, the point of this one is different.)

Activity

Have an arm wrestling contest in your family. Take turns seeing who can beat Dad. Or you might want to have some fun lifting weights to see how strong everybody is. If your family keeps track of how much everyone grows, take a look at the measurements to see how much everyone changes year to year. In one of these ways or another one you might think of, make the point that everyone is growing, maturing and changing.

APPLicatien

Gideon is an interesting character. To some he might have seemed like a weak little kid, but God saw much more in him and used him for amazing things. Read through Judges 6 together. It is a longer reading than most devotionals, but it is a great story. This was a dark, scary time in the history of the Israelites. (Side lesson: doing evil in God's eyes will always get you in trouble.)

The Midianites had invaded the land and impoverished God's people. When God comes to talk to Gideon, he is threshing wheat in a winepress, hiding to keep it from the Midianites. God tries to encourage Gideon, telling him that the Lord is with him and calling him a mighty warrior. Read Gideon's reaction in verse 13.

What is Gideon saying to God? Think of the stories that Gideon has grown up hearing about how God had led the Israelites and had worked wonders and miraculous things among them. What is Gideon's attitude? He wants to know what's going on now. He's heard all these great things, but he hasn't experienced anything like these himself.

Now read God's response in verse 14. God never even addresses anything from the past, but tells Gideon to go as he is and save Israel out of Midian's hand. Then God reminds Gideon that the Lord is sending him. This is a great lesson for our kids. They may have heard us tell a lot of stories about how God has worked in our lives, and they may have seen a lot of things for themselves. But seeing God work in someone else's life is not the same as experiencing it yourself.

God basically tells Gideon that the past doesn't matter, what his family has experienced doesn't matter, but all that matters is the plan that God has for his own life.

Ask how Gideon might be feeling right then, knowing that God wants to use him to do something that no one else has been able to do. In verse 15 we can see that Gideon is scared. Talk about how it can be scary to grow up and get ready to go out on your own. (By middle school, most kids have already started experiencing teachers talking to them about what they plan to do after school, getting ready for college, etc. This is not a new topic for them).

The cool thing about God is how he worked with Gideon all through this chapter to help him grow in his faith and get prepared to finally go into battle and do all that God needed him to do. Gideon built his own personal relationship with God by listening to him and deciding to obey God even when it was hard. Encourage your children that just as God worked with Gideon, he will also work with each of them, giving them opportunities to grow and getting them ready to face whatever he has planned for their future.

Plans, Commitments or Follow Up

Ask each of your children during the next week how they felt about this devotional. Ask them what things seem scary about growing up and how reading about Gideon might have helped them. Encourage them to take small steps consistently in growing closer to God, listening to his word and praying for the courage and strength to obey just like Gideon did.

Scripture Memory or Additional Study

Psalm 18:32–33

25

Gotta Have God's Word!

1 Peter 2:2–3

Objective

By helping your children to understand the drive to eat that a young baby has, you will also help them to understand the kind of drive that God wants us to have to "feed" on his word. You will also pull your family closer together as you look at pictures from the past.

Activity

Bring out pictures of each of your children as small babies. It seems that kids never tire of seeing pictures of themselves and marveling that they were ever that small. Let them discuss the pictures. If any of your children are old enough to remember the birth of a brother or sister, let them share about what they remember.

Tell them how as babies they let you know when they were hungry. Imitate their loud insistent cry that would pierce the air (and your eardrums).

Ask them why that drive is so powerful. What would happen if the need for food was not met? Ask them if they have seen the sad pictures of starving children from Africa or other countries? Those pictures show what happens if a child does not have the food he needs.

APPLication

Read aloud the text for this devotional (1 Peter 2:2–3). Ask the children what this text means, what it is saying.

It drives home the point that we need to be eager or desperate for God's word in our lives as a newborn baby is eager or desperate for milk (that is, we need to "crave pure spiritual milk").

- How does that spiritual milk help us to "grow up in our salvation"?
- What does it mean that we as human beings need "spiritual food"?
- How do we get that spiritual food? What if we don't get spiritual food? (Our growth is stunted, we don't develop properly on the inside, in our heart where God wants to live.)
- What do you think happened to your cries for food when Mom started nursing you or gave you a bottle? (They were silent. From a mother's perspective it is such a blessed quietness after the desperate screaming.)
- Why is a baby quiet when he is being fed? (His need is being met. He is content, satisfied, at peace.)
- If we "feed" on God's word, how does it affect us in much the same way that you were affected as a baby when you got fed?
- Why do we sometimes not eat spiritual food (not spend time reading God's word)?
- How can we encourage each other as a family to keep getting our spiritual food?

PLans, CoMMitMents oR FoLLoW-UP

Let each child choose one picture of him or her as a baby. Put the chosen pictures on the refrigerator or somewhere they will be seen during the coming week. Let them serve as a reminder to "crave pure spiritual milk," to read God's word during this week.

SCRiPtURe MeMoRY oR ADDitioNaL StUDY

Psalm 119:103

26

CREATOR AND CREATION

Romans 1:20

OBJECTIVE

Just because we take our children to church and read the Bible with them doesn't mean that they don't have questions and doubts they need to wrestle with in developing their own faith. The preteen years especially can be a time our children are deciding if everything they have heard and seen at home and church over the years is true. This devotional is one way of opening a dialogue with our kids to help them on their journey to faith.

ACTIVITY

Have everyone in the family draw a picture of their favorite thing in nature. If your family isn't very artistic, maybe you would want to look through magazines or books and pick out photos instead. Take turns telling each other why you chose what you did and why it is so special to you.

APPLICATION

Read Romans 1:20 and discuss its meaning. How have God's eternal power and divine nature been clearly seen? How does seeing what God has made give us understanding of God?

Ask your children if they believe God created the earth. How do we know that he did?

Use the following analogy to discuss this topic: Think about if you were walking in the woods one day and found a watch. (Look at a watch.) How would you think that the watch got there? Did it "grow" from the ground? Did someone make it?

Why do you think that there has to be a "maker" for the watch?

Look around at something that God has made—your brother, your skin, your dog, etc. Look at yourself in the mirror, walk outside and look around. Did all that you see just happen to "grow" by chance or did someone make it?

Why do you think that God created the world rather than it just happening?

PLANS, COMMITMENTS OR FOLLOW UP

Pray together as a family, thanking God for all that he has made and praising him for the creativity he has displayed for us. In addition, take time during the following week to have private, individual discussions on this subject with each of your children. While they may not have questions about God creating the world, it may bring up other questions that they do have. They may feel more comfortable discussing those things in private, rather than during a family devotional time.

SCRIPTURE MEMORY OR ADDITIONAL STUDY

Psalm 19:1–4

27

MakinG Wise Decisions

Proverbs 3:21–24, Philippians 1:9–11

OBJective

Teaching our children to make good decisions is one of the most important things we do as parents. When they are young, we make most of the decisions for them, but as they grow older, we must allow our children the space to begin to make more decisions and learn from the consequences, both good and bad. This devotional is aimed at giving our kids tools to use in thinking through decisions they face.

ActivitY

(Supplies: 1 yardstick)

Some decisions are easy to make, others are more difficult. Sometimes we have to look ahead to what might happen rather than just look at what is right in front of us or what is easiest.

Have one person try to balance the yardstick *straight up* in the palm of their hand, looking ONLY at their hand. (They will not be able to do this without crazy wobbling and maneuvering.) Then have someone else try to balance it the same way, looking at the TOP of the stick. (Much better control and balance.)

APPLication

Have one person read Proverbs 3:21–24 and another read Philippians 1:9–11. Discuss what it means to "discern what is best" and how a person can "preserve sound judgment and discernment." "Discern" means to know or to figure out. "Sound judgment" is about making good and wise decisions.

We all face many decisions every day. For example, we decide to either get up when the alarm goes off in the morning or to turn over and go back to sleep. We make decisions about what to eat and whether to watch television when we get home from school or work, or whether to do homework, call friends, clean up around the house, exercise, etc.

We also face decisions to go along with the crowd at school, to swear, to make jokes that are lewd or hurtful, and to find websites that have sexual content, to smoke or try drugs. The situation that is right in front of us may seem like the easiest or most fun thing to do. It is helpful if we look at "the end of the matter" in order to make the right choices.

True story: *There was a young man who started smoking when he was thirteen years old. He didn't think it would ever hurt him or cause him any trouble. He thought it was pretty cool and fought with his parents about it. Years later, when he was thirty years old, he had a beautiful wife and a young son who was his delight. But now he also had lung cancer, and soon after being diagnosed, he died. He never realized how this one bad decision would cause him so much physical pain and would casue those he loved to be left alone and in great emotional pain.*

Do you think if he could go back to thirteen years old, he would choose differently? Why?

Every decision we make has a consequence, good or bad. Some things, like getting up late once in a while, may not seem like a big deal. Over time, though, if we continue to roll over when the alarm goes off, our character becomes lazy, and we may end up having a hard time getting or keeping a job.

Discuss some decisions each family member has faced lately. Talk about how to make good and wise decisions. Will my decision help me grow closer to God? Will my decision help or hurt my character in any way? Will my decision hurt anyone else? (Sometimes even making a wise decision will hurt others, if they don't agree with or like what you are doing.) Does the outcome of my decision have lasting positive or negative consequences?

Plans, Commitments or Follow Up

Philippians teaches us that when we discern what is best (and decide to take action on what is best), we can be blameless and spotless before God. Commit as a family to pray daily about all kinds of decisions we make. We don't need to agonize or over-analyze each and every decision, but if we will pray and think every day about the path we are choosing, God will direct us and show us what is the best way. We also learn from making the wrong choices, which is a valuable lesson. This topic is one that will provide much discussion over time. It is helpful to lay the foundation to open channels for communication as our children grow and continue to face new and interesting decisions.

Scripture Memory or Additional Study

Psalm 37:5–6

GOD WANTS YOU!

Romans 5:6-8, Matthew 23:37

OBJECTIVE

Our God loves us with a strong love and longs to have a relationship with us! He sent Jesus to die for us when we were still powerless. He calls out to us over and over again. Too often we read the Bible as a book of rules and regulations, showing us what we need to do to obey God.

While God has written down his laws for us to learn and obey, the Bible is a love story showing God reaching out to his people over and over again, seeking a relationship with them. This devotional is aimed at looking at how much God longs to be close to us.

ACTIVITY

Take turns sharing about a special event in each person's life. Ask everyone to share what made it special and to describe their feelings about the event. Mom and Dad may want to share about dating and falling in love. Share how you knew Mom was the right woman for you, how being with her made you feel (and vice versa).

What is it like when someone treats you special and plans something that they know will make you feel like "royalty."

APPLiCATiON

We don't always spend a lot of time thinking about how amazing it is that God wants a special, unique relationship with each one of us. Read Romans 5:6–8 and discuss how much God longed to have a relationship with his created beings.

What was God willing to give to show his love for us?

We can feel unworthy and have trouble accepting that God would have given Jesus up even if we were the only person in the world, but it is a very true statement.

At just the right time, when we couldn't do anything to make ourselves pure in God's eyes, he demonstrated his love for us by giving up his one and only Son! God went all out in his demonstration!

Ask your children if they believe this. Ask how it makes them feel to think that God did that just for them. God didn't give up Jesus to make us feel guilty, but in order to provide the way to heaven and give us the best life possible on this earth.

Then read Matthew 23:37. Describe how a mother hen gathers her little chicks under her wings to protect them when they are in danger or even just when they are afraid. (If your kids would enjoy it, act this out with them. Cluck around and gather them under your arms.)

In this passage, God says he wanted to gather the people under his wings, but what happened? (They would not let him; they ran away.) Why do you think they did not want to come to God? How did it make him feel that they didn't want to come to him? How do you think it makes him feel when we do come to him and let him gather us under his wing to care for us and to protect us?

Ask how it makes everyone feel to know that God has this love for each individual? If we were to walk around thinking about God's love and these passages every day, how would it change the way we live?

PLANS, COMMiTMENTS OR FOLLOW UP

Take turns praying and thanking God for his love for each one of us. Remind your children every day how much God loves them and how much he really wants to reach out to them and help them in their lives. Post the scriptures that mean the most to your family in a place that can be seen every day as everyone walks out the door.

You might even want to find a picture of a mother hen with her chicks to put up on the refrigerator for the next week as a reminder of God's love for us.

SCRIPTURE MEMORY OR ADDITIONAL STUDY

3 John 1:4

Satan wants You Too!

2 Corinthians 2:11, Ephesians 6:11, 13–17

OBjective

It is important that we teach our children about the spiritual battle going on for our souls every day. While God desires to have a relationship with us, Satan hates us and tries constantly to pull us away from God. This devotional is designed to help teach your children to be on the lookout for Satan's schemes, so that he loses any power to lure them away from seeking a close relationship with God.

Activity

Watch a documentary on lions as a family. There are often shows about cats on the National Geographic channel, or you may be able to check one out from your local library. If you can't locate one, check out a book about lions from the library to look through at the beginning of this devotional.

Discuss how lions and cats in general sneak up on their prey. They are very careful and quiet and take one little step at a time so that their target does not even notice. Lions are very patient. They watch herds for hours, locating the slowest, oldest, youngest or injured member of the pack. They always find the weakest animal to attack, one that can't run away or fight back.

APPLICation

Read 2 Corinthians 2:11 and Ephesians 6:11 out loud. The Bible teaches us that Satan is scheming, that he has a plan to attack each one of us. Discuss how Satan can be like the lion. Would he be more likely to attack us when we are strong or when we are weak in our faith? If Satan is always scheming to get us to disobey God, what might some of those schemes or plans be? Would it be the same plan for every person? Just like the lion watches his prey to find the weakest place to attack, so Satan watches us and tries to figure out the area we would be most vulnerable in.

While it is important to identify how Satan might try to attack us, it is equally important to remember that when we put on the full armor of God, we will always be strong enough to resist and stand against the devil's schemes.

Let's discuss some ways that Satan might try to pull us away from God. For example, discuss how Satan tries to keep us from reading the Bible. How does that keep us from growing in our faith? Why would Satan want to keep us from reading?

Parents, it is important that you study your children and help them identify ways Satan tries to keep them from obeying God. If your child struggles with wanting to look good all the time, Satan might try to tempt them to lie or to cheat at school. If "the world" looks very attractive to your child, Satan will send them friends to try to draw them into that scene. The devil can also use conflicts with friends at church to keep our kids from wanting to obey the Bible and be close to God.

If we find it hard to forgive, Satan will make sure that we get hurt often by friends or family members. Satan will use anything he can to lure us away.

Read Ephesians 6:13–17, and discuss the different parts of the full armor of God and how "putting on" this armor can help each person to fight Satan's schemes. You can even have your kids act out putting each part on as you read the scripture.

End this devotional by reading 1 John 4:4 together. Remind your family that God is stronger than Satan and that if we are trying to follow and obey God, he will protect us from the devil. God will always help us overcome if we resist Satan. We can't resist something we don't understand, however, so that is why this is an important topic to discuss as a family.

Plans, Commitments or Follow Up

Keep a Bible and a belt on the kitchen table during the week as a reminder to everyone that the Bible is the "belt of truth" that will help everyone overcome any scheme that Satan uses to pull us away from God. Talk individually with each of your children to make sure they understand that this is a subject to be sober about, but not to be afraid of. God will always give us victory in our lives.

Scripture Memory or Additional Study

Matthew 4:10

SUCCESSFUL FAILINGS

2 Corinthians 1:8–11

OBJECTIVE

It is true that no one likes to face hard times. It is also true that everyone will face hard times. The standards of following Jesus are high, and God wants excellence from all of us, but it is unrealistic to think that we will always handle difficult times well.

Paul faced difficult times and had to be reminded that God was in control. He had to learn that when he felt he could not endure the pressure, God would give him the strength.

God wants to shower his grace and forgiveness on us during the hard times we face, but we need to learn how to make these times as successful as possible.

ACTIVITY

We believe that as parents, it is important for us to share not only the victories we experience, but the difficulties as well. One time we were sharing with a Christian brother about some things that were hard for us when we first moved to Kenya to be part of the church planting. He encouraged us to write everything down for our kids so that they could learn from all we went through. It was a good lesson for us. We had never thought to tell the kids about the challenges we faced.

Use this time to be open with your kids about something in your life that didn't go the way you would have wanted. Perhaps you failed a course in high school or college, perhaps a sin has been hard for you to overcome, or a relationship has been really challenging. Be sensitive to the ages and maturity of your kids as you share, giving details accordingly.

Share about how you handled the situation, what you would have done differently and what you learned from it.

APPLicatien

Talk about how every person faces things that are hard during the course of their life. It might seem to us that it would be nice to just breeze through life with no problems, no setbacks, no temptations, but that is just not realistic. Also, it would not help us to know how much we need God.

We are sinners who need God's grace and mercy every day as we fall short in our efforts to imitate Jesus. But failing or sinning doesn't make us failures. Satan wants us to hide and be ashamed of sin or failure; God wants to forgive us.

In 2 Corinthians 1:8–11, Paul wanted the whole Corinthian church to know about the hardships he was facing. He said the pressure was so great that he thought they were going to die! But Paul's perspective on everything was so refreshing. He was open and asked everyone to pray for them. He didn't minimize the challenges, but also recognized that what he was facing had happened so that he might learn to rely on God.

Perhaps if he had been more humble in the first place, he wouldn't have had to face such difficulties to learn to rely on God. Or perhaps God just wanted to take him to a deeper level of dependence. Either way, Paul could have just kept silent, suffering though the lessons he was learning.

Instead he chose to ask a whole church to pray for him. What can we learn from Paul?

How does God want us to react when we are under pressure, when we sin, when something we try isn't working out positively? God wants us to be open and honest, to share with others and to ask for help.

Read 1 John 1:5–7.

If we are involved in sin, God wants us to come into the light and share about it. He promises that if we come into the light, we will have fellowship with one another and Jesus' blood will purify us from all unrighteousness.

If our failure doesn't come from sin (for example, we study for a test but fail because we just don't understand the material) we need to ask for help and just be honest and open so that we don't end up walking into another of Satan's traps: pride and trying to look good.

Plans, Commitments or Follow Up

Ask your kids if there is anything they would like to talk about or need help with. Ask if they feel comfortable discussing things with you, or if they are afraid to be open for fear of disappointing you. Make sure your kids know you will always listen and try to respond to everything in a godly way. Reassure them that you will always love them and be proud of who they are, that those things don't come as a result of them always "winning" or doing everything right.

Scripture Memory or Additional Study

Matthew 11:28–29, Romans 8:1

REMEMBER!

1 Chronicles 16:7–14

OBJECTIVE

This devotional is designed to give your family an opportunity to reflect on and to remember all the ways God has blessed you—individually and as a family. It always builds our faith and joy to remember what God has done in our lives. It is even encouraging to remember difficult times and how they produced changes, deeper convictions or molded our character.

ACTIVITY

There are a few ways you could introduce this devotional. You might want to pull out family photos. Going back through photos is a great way to remember significant moments in your family's history. When our family does this, it always seems to lead to remembering other details about a trip we took or an event that is recorded. It also causes us to remember friends and family members.

Another way you might introduce this devo is to write up a short quiz. Write or say a date or event, and have everyone share what they remember about what happened.

Or write several significant events on separate pieces of paper. Fold them up and put them in a hat. Take turns choosing and sharing about whatever is written on the paper. After each person shares, let the other family member fill in details about what they remember.

APPLication

Ask someone to read from 1 Chronicles 16:7–14. Talk about how wonderful our God is and how much he blesses our lives every day.

Discuss ways we can give praise to God by remembering how much he has blessed us. It helps us to be more thankful when we remember and talk about how God has worked in our lives.

Verse 11 reminds us to look to the Lord and to seek his strength and his face always. Discuss how your family has learned to seek God and to rely on him during both good and challenging times.

Parents, you might want to share things from your childhood or from being a young adult—situations God used to teach you something important about your character or about life in general.

In verse 10 David says to "glory in God's holy name, to let the hearts of those who seek the Lord rejoice." Ask everyone to share how they feel about God right now as they are remembering wonderful times, lessons learned and how God has blessed them. It brings us closer to God and makes us appreciate him and each other more when we dwell on these positive thoughts and memories.

Plans, Commitments or Follow-up

Pray together at the end of the devotional, thanking and praising God for all the wonderful ways He has blessed you and your family. During the following week, ask each other daily for any other memories that popped into your mind during the day. Dinner time might be a great time to continue discussing God's blessings, both in the past and during that day as well.

Scripture Memory or Additional Study

Psalm 100:4–5

TRiUMPHant TRansitions

Joshua 1:1–9

OBJective

Transition or times of change can be challenging for our children. Some people thrive on change while others cower inside at the thought of making new friends, learning new things or finding their way around in new surroundings. This devotional is designed to help us keep our children and family focused on God's promise of victory during those times.

ACtivitY

Take time as a family to discuss whatever transition is happening currently, or a time of change that may be approaching. Ask each family member to share how they are feeling about the change and what they think the change will mean to them—both good things and scary things.

Right now in our family we have a son who will be a senior and a daughter who will go to high school next year. We also have a family business that is growing, and we have the need to hire and train new employees. We find it helpful for several reasons to take time to discuss all kinds of changes that happen.

First, it helps us to prepare mentally for what is about to happen. Second, it helps us to know what each person is thinking and expecting, which cuts down on friction and misunderstandings later on. Third, we can pray together about the changes, which teach us all to rely on God and to trust him to give us victories. Last, it helps each of us to think of positive solutions to any problems that may arise during the transition.

APPLicatiPn

Read Joshua 1:1–9 together. Discuss the transition Joshua was facing: becoming the leader of all the Israelites. Ask everyone to share how they think he might have been feeling about taking on this new task. Discuss some of the challenges he might have been facing.

Then discuss God's "pep talk" with Joshua. How does God encourage Joshua? How does he challenge him? What does God expect from him during this time of change? What does God promise Joshua?

Apply everyone's answers to the specific change or transition that is going on in your family. What does God expect from us during times of change? What does God promise us? How can we apply these scriptures to our own situations? Is anything hard for us to believe in our own situation?

It is really important to help everyone in the family be honest. We may read a passage like Joshua 1 and have these great feelings of victory...until we start applying them to our own lives.

God commands Joshua to hold tightly to the Book of the Law and not to turn from it to the left or to the right. Discuss how holding tightly to God's word during times of change helps us be victorious.

In verse 3 God promises to give Joshua every place he sets his foot. Try to visualize together what that will mean for each family member during the upcoming or ongoing change. Where will everyone be setting their feet? How might they expect to be victorious in those situations? What challenges might they face? (Joshua and the Israelites still had to go out and fight for the land—it wasn't just handed over.) How might God use the changes or transitions to mold our character?

PLans, CPMMitMents PR FPLLPW UP

Have everyone find a scripture during the week to share with the family about being victorious during times of change (younger children will need some help with this). Post them on the refrigerator or other place so that everyone can read them daily and be encouraged. Pray together about the changes and continue to talk openly about how everyone is feeling. Being open and honest with one another is one of the important ways for us to stay close to God and also close to each other.

SCRiPTURe MeMORY OR ADDitiOnal STUDY

Psalm 18:28–29

WATCH YOUR WORDS!

Proverbs 12:18

OBJECTIVE

What we say has the potential to be helpful or to do harm. We should be careful about what we say since we can create many problems if we don't exercise great care. This devotional explores the importance of choosing our words wisely.

ACTIVITY

Select an open space on the floor and lay down some old newspapers to protect the surface. Give each family member turns squeezing out the contents of a one big tube of toothpaste onto the floor.

APPLICATION

Read Proverbs 12:18. This passage is very challenging. Point out to your family that God uses such passages to remind us to be very careful about the words we use when we communicate with others. To help your children to understand the word "reckless," ask them to describe a reckless driver. Then make the application to a reckless communicator.

Discuss that when we use toothpaste correctly (to brush our teeth) it does us a lot of good. It keeps our teeth clean, prevents cavities and makes our mouths smell good.

However, if we use it incorrectly (e.g., squeezing it on the floor), we can no longer use it for its intended purpose. It actually creates quite a mess for us to clean up later on!

In the same way, if we are not careful in choosing our words, we can find ourselves having to clean up big messes in our lives. Reckless words are words that are not used for their intended purpose; they end up hurting others.

Ask your children to try putting the toothpaste back into the tube after scraping it off the newspaper. Let them try for a few minutes; then ask a few questions.

Is it hard to get the toothpaste back into the tube? What are the chances of being able to get it all back into the tube?

If we are not careful in choosing our words, we can find ourselves in a situation just like we are in now, as we try to put this toothpaste back into the tube. We can't really take back our words, and we will have hurt ourselves and others by the careless use of our words.

Ask everyone if they have ever had a time that they regretted saying something to someone. Discuss how it made them feel to know they had hurt someone. Discuss how the other person felt as well.

Ask how they have felt when someone hurt them by the careless choice of words. Parents, this is a great opportunity to share examples from your own lives that your children can relate to. This is also a great time for everyone in the family to think about how they have been speaking to each other and to apologize to and forgive each other.

Use this time to discuss appropriate ways to express different thoughts and feelings that we all experience. Think of ways to express hurt feelings, anger and frustration without casting blame, but by simply expressing how you feel. This is a great time to teach your family the principle of not using the words "never" or "always" when responding to each other (e.g., "You never let me..., or you always...").

Plans, Commitments or Follow Up

Pray together about speaking to each other and everyone else in a way that will be pleasing to God. Be thankful that God gives us reminders of the difficult consequences that reckless words can bring. Encourage each other as you notice positive changes in your family's speech.

SCRIPTURE MEMORY OR ADDITIONAL STUDY

Proverbs 15:1

EATING FOR GOOD HEALTH

Psalm 139:14, 1 Corinthians 6:19–20

OBJECTIVE

Our bodies are "fearfully and wonderfully made," and Jesus directs us to take care of our bodies, which are the temple of God. The messages we send to our children are important because in today's world, we're all sent many conflicting messages about our bodies: what they should look like, what "healthy" is, and how to improve your health. This devotional helps us focus as a family on eating in a healthy manner.

ACTIVITY

Have each family member write down their idea of a healthy family meal. After everyone is finished, take turns reading the menus out loud. Have each family member share why they consider the meal they "prepared" to be healthy. Ask each person to describe "healthy" in their own words. What picture does that word conjure up in their minds?

APPLICATION

Read Psalm 139:14 and 1 Corinthians 6:19–20 together. Discuss how God feels about our bodies and why we should take good care of ourselves. Discuss how food plays a role in our being healthy and strong.

While "healthy" may mean different things to different people, there are a few things that should be included in meals to make them nutritionally sound and good for our bodies. How popular are fruits and vegetables in your home? Which is easier for everyone in your home—eating a slice of pizza or a serving of spinach?

For most of us, the answer is obvious. Children and adolescents will naturally be drawn to sweets or "kid-friendly" foods such as macaroni and cheese, pizza, and French fries. Vegetables, on the other hand, can be more difficult to learn to like or at least to tolerate.

Teaching our children to try new foods without having a fit, learning to accept most foods and politely saying "no thank you" to the rest will come in very handy later in life! It may take ten to twenty tastes before we learn to like a certain food. With practice, we can teach our children to become more confident in their ability to master unfamiliar foods. These are important life skills by which adults are often judged in social settings. At the same time, eating a variety of foods is important for all of us to get essential nutrients that our bodies need to stay healthy.

If your family is already eating a balanced diet, encourage each other to keep making healthy choices at school and work, in addition to family meals at home. If your family needs to make some changes, discuss steps to take together. Discuss things that keep everyone from making healthy choices.

Mom and Dad, do you enjoy eating fruits and vegetables? We make things easier for our children when we model what we want from them. Just as in other aspects of our lives, eating well and taking care of our bodies is part of being a follower of Jesus.

Our culture often doesn't help us in this area. It encourages working late, family members eating separately whenever they are hungry, often in various rooms of the house or in front of the TV. Sports and activities are often carelessly scheduled during dinner hours.

Discuss what steps your family can take to change any eating habits that need to be changed. Perhaps you can decide to try one new food a week. If your children are old enough, perhaps they can begin to plan and prepare one meal a week that incorporates a new food. If the whole family is involved, this plan can be a great adventure, rather than a chore.

Plans, Commitments or Follow Up

Write down three steps your family will take in the next month to work toward taking care of your bodies and putting healthy foods in your diets. Some ideas might be to include a fruit at breakfast and lunch, to eat one new vegetable each week or to learn a new way to prepare a vegetable the family already enjoys.

Another idea would be to turn off the television at every meal or snack so that you can focus on the food you are eating and really enjoy the bounty that God has given us.

Scripture Memory or Additional Study

1 Timothy 6:17
Genesis 1:29

FRUiT OF REPENTANCE

Luke 3:7–14

OBJECTIVE

When we change our heart, we change our behavior. This devotional helps us learn how our behavior reflects our hearts and what we can do to change.

ACTIVITY

For younger children: Have two drawings of trees ready for the devotional. Ask your children to take turns drawing and coloring "bad apples" on the first tree. Discuss what kind of trees produce "bad apples." Then take turns drawing and coloring good apples on the second tree. Likewise, discuss the attributes of a good tree that produces good apples.

For older children: Set out a bowl of fruit and invite everyone to choose a piece to eat during the devotional. Mix good and spoiled fruit. Watch and note everyone's reactions. (You might want to buy some bananas several days before the devotional. They will "over ripen" fast!)

APPLICATION

Read Luke 3:7–14. John the Baptist came before Jesus to prepare people's hearts to receive the message that Jesus would bring them. God's goal in all this was that all people would see the salvation of God (verse 6). John's message was very direct and challenging, telling the crowds that they must show their repentance by their deeds and not by words alone. Consider verses 7–9.

Talk as a family about what it means to bear fruit that proves your repentance. If your children are older and you set out fruit to eat, discuss why no one chose to eat the spoiled or over ripe fruit. Discuss what makes that kind of fruit unappealing.

Ask what would be going on in our lives if we were bearing spoiled fruit. Discuss what repentance means: a change in direction, a change in actions. When you sin or make a mistake, how will the people around you know that you have repented? If you lied about something and you repent, will you continue to lie? How is saying "I'm sorry" different from repenting? When the Israelites said "we have Abraham as a father," it is like saying today "we belong to a great church." Going to a great church isn't the same thing as having a good heart. What is the difference? How does our behavior reflect our hearts?

Read verses 10–14 again. Discuss how John encouraged the people to show that they had repented. Notice how all types of people came to John to find out about getting closer to God. All of us are different, have different interests, hobbies, jobs, etc. But notice how God has a plan for each person to change.

Ask each family member to share one thing they think they need to repent of in their lives. Parents, we would encourage you to start the sharing and model honesty and humility before your children.

Plans, Commitments or Follow Up

Write down the one thing that each family member shared that they want to repent of and post it in a place that the family can see, but that is not public for everyone who walks into your home. Commit to pray for each other and to encourage each other as you see everyone making the desired changes. Remind everyone how pleased God is when we change because of a desire to be closer to him.

SCRIPTURE MEMORY OR ADDITIONAL STUDY

Matthew 12:33

36

GOOD GIFTS FROM THE FATHER

Matthew 7:7–11

OBJECTIVE

This devotional will demonstrate in a surprising way that God gives good gifts to his children. He does not delight in tricking us or playing games with us. He is always eager to take care of us and give us what we truly need.

ACTIVITY

Get a box, and put a rock in it. Then wrap the box to look like a beautiful and inviting gift. Also wrap some candy or cookies or other dessert that your kids like.

Keep the second gift hidden, and give the first gift to your children. Draw straws in some way (flip a coin) to see who is going to get to open it.

APPLICATION

When they open it and see that is it is just a rock, that you tricked them, read Matthew 7:7–11.

Ask the kids how they felt when they saw the gift at first. Then ask them how they felt when they opened it.

Remind them that you just did this to make a point, that you always want them to be able to trust you. You want what is best for them, and you want to give them good gifts. And this is the way God is toward us.

Ask the children if they can remember any answered prayers in your family's lives. Be ready to share some yourself if they can't come up with any. Remind them that these answers were gifts from God.

Share about how you have learned to trust God with your needs and with your family's needs.

End the devotional by bringing out the other gift. Ask one of the children to read verses 9–11.

Even though you are not perfect yourself ("evil"), as a parent, you always want to give good gifts to your kids. And how much more does God, who is perfect, want to give good gifts to his kids.

Let the children open the present, and then share the yummy treat with the whole family.

Plans, Commitments or Follow Up

Tell your children that you are going to put the rock in the middle of the table for the next week. Then every night when you sit down to eat dinner, you can remind each other of this passage and how good God is to us as his children.

Scripture Memory or Additional Study

Luke 11:13

37

OVERCOMING THE FEAR FACTOR

1 Samuel 13:1–15

OBJECTIVE

Fear is a dangerous animal that leads us to act in ways that are often harmful to ourselves and everyone around us as well. This devotional explores how fear can trigger certain responses from us and also helps us think of ways as a family to overcome fear and become more faithful.

ACTIVITY

Ask everyone to share something that they have seen someone do that they would be afraid to do. Why would they be afraid? What would they fear would happen to them?

Talk about different fears that are common to people: fear of snakes or spiders, or fear of heights, or fear of speaking in front of crowds. Talk about how some fears don't necessarily affect your daily life, but others can make people change the way they live and act. For example, some people have a fear of open spaces (agoraphobia) and so they never leave their homes.

APPLicatiꞮn

Read 1 Samuel 13:1–15. Talk about what a difficult situation Saul is in here. Ask how they would feel if members of your family had to face something similar to Saul. How would it feel to know that everyone around you was afraid and was leaving the battle? It was a difficult place to be. What are some difficult situations we face that can tempt us to react in fear like Saul did?

One area we might not think about immediately is facing conflict in our families. Saul's fear led to a chain of events that eventually cost him the kingdom. Think of a time that there was conflict in your family. Discuss how fear might have played a role in the conflict. Sometimes as parents we can over-react because we are fearful that our children are not listening to us, or that they are not being respectful or obedient.

In turn, sometimes our children can become defensive because they are fearful that they won't be listened to or that their opinions don't count. When those fears take over, how does that lead to conflict?

If Saul had been humble and trusted the plan that Samuel had laid out, how might the outcome of this situation been different? In the same way, when conflicts arise at home, how can humility and trust work to change the tone of our interactions with each other?

Discuss how fear changed the course of Saul's life and how fear can change our lives as well. Fear can make us pull back and become silent, or it can also produce the opposite effect and make us defensive and angry and loud.

Fear can also keep us from being open and honest with our friends and family. Ask your children how you can change to make it easier for them to discuss things with you. Share with them what reactions you would appreciate in return. If everyone in the family works on listening and being humble with each other, trusting that each wants the best for the other, everyone will learn to overcome their fears, and home can be the safe place God intended it to be.

PLans, CꞮMMitments ꞮR FꞮllꞮW UP

Take time during the next week to spend time with each of your children and discuss how they felt about this devotional. Ask if there is anything they would like to talk about from the past that would help your communication be better. Pray together during the week for everyone to overcome their fears and learn to listen and respect and love each other.

SCRIPTURE MEMORY OR ADDITIONAL STUDY

Psalm 37:3–4, 7–8

38

GOD IS a GOD OF ORDER

Numbers 4

OBJECTIVE

For a family to function day to day together in a harmonious and efficient way, there needs to be some order. This is true in keeping the house clean and uncluttered, and in scheduling and communicating with each other so there is not chaos everywhere. This devotional shows how ordered God was with the Israelites when they were living in the desert for forty years, traveling on foot and camping in different places all the time.

ACTIVITY

Tell your kids that to prepare for today's devotional, you are all going to move from one room to another. There are certain items that will need to go with you to the other room: the table lamp, the Bibles, pillows to sit on, and any other items you want to include (even if they are random).

Then make the point that you don't want people just grabbing this or that. That would not be a very ordered approach, and something might be left behind. So, assign specific items to each person to take to the other room. Make sure they know their assignments and any instructions that go with it (for example: [1] turn off the lamp and unplug it first. Then when we get to the other room, put it on the floor, plug it in and turn it on. [2] put the pillows in a circle, etc.)

Once everyone has their assignments, say, "Okay, let's move out. Everyone bring what they were assigned to bring."

When you get to the other room, expect everyone to set things up the way they were instructed. After sitting there a few minutes, say, "Now, we need to move to another room. All of us know our assignments." Then get up and go to another room. After you are totally set up there, settle in to have your devotional (or you could even go to one other room if you like).

APPLication

God's special people in the Old Testament were the Israelites. When he set them free from slavery in Egypt, he led them in the desert for forty years before he gave them their new home.

The people traveled and camped different places all that time. God would let them know when it was time to move, and they moved immediately.

God is a God of order. We can know that just by looking at the ordered universe he created. We see his order in Numbers 25–27 where he instructs the Israelites how to build the tabernacle that was his special place to live among them.

Look at Numbers 4 (for example verses 5–6 and 29–32). God gives instructions to the different clans of the Levites for moving the tabernacle from place to place. Each person had his particular task. Every time the Israelites pulled up camp, each Levite knew exactly what his responsibility was, exactly what he needed to carry to the new location and how he was to set it up when they got there. Even to the detail of carrying the tent pegs, they had their specific assignments.

Ask the kids why this was the best approach. What would have happened if they had not had such specific assignments? Ask them to describe what it could have looked like. (They would have been grabbing curtains and altars and scrambling to take the tent down. They would have been yelling—"Hey, who is getting the tent pegs? I got them last time, and I don't want to get them this time. They get my hands dirty!" etc.) You might even want to have some fun and act out the chaos that could have occurred.

Reflect on your "moves" earlier in the activity. What did the kids learn from that about the importance of order?

111

Close the devo reminding everyone that God is a God of order, and in the family everyone needs to do their part to keep things running smoothly. Discuss what some of those things are: cleaning up after ourselves, not leaving dishes in the den, talking ahead of time about the schedule of events for the week, or whatever is needed in your household.

Plans, Commitments or Follow-Up

Remind everyone to take items you moved back where they belong. If you have time you might want to watch *Prince of Egypt* together to remember about how God worked in an ordered way to bring his people out of slavery (or plan to watch it over the weekend). Have one or all of the kids write out a sign, "Remember the tent pegs." Put the sign on the refrigerator for the next week as a reminder to everyone to do their part to have order in the house.

Scripture Memory or Additional Study

Genesis 1:14–15

39

EXEMPLARY WORK HABITS

> Daniel 6:1–5

OBJECTIVE

During the teen years, many of our children will begin to work for the first time. This devotional can help us get them ready to face new responsibilities diligently and with integrity. (And if you children are not old enough to be thinking about getting a job, apply this devotional to their responsibilities around the house and in school.)

ACTIVITY

Start this devotional with some play acting. Have one person be the boss (from a grocery store or an ice cream parlor). He/she asks another person to do certain tasks—put inventory on the shelves, sweep the floors, bag groceries, wash the dishes, etc. First have the second person act out doing what was asked with a good attitude. Then have them act it out either by not performing the tasks at all or by doing it but complaining the whole time.

You can apply the same idea to performing certain tasks at home: doing homework, cleaning their room, doing the dishes—whatever applies to your kids.

APPLICATiON

Share with your children about the first jobs that you had when you were near their ages. Tell them both what you enjoyed (if you can remember back then) and what was challenging to you.

Read from Daniel 6:1–5. Discuss Daniel's character. What was he like on the job? How did he compare to others that held similar positions? What made Daniel different? How did his peers feel about his example and character? Did their feelings or attitudes affect Daniel in any way? Why or why not?

Apply these same questions to jobs that your children have now or are thinking of applying for. Discuss what it means to have integrity and to be diligent. Why is being honest and trustworthy important as an employee? Considering the jobs, discuss how your children can show diligence and a hard-working spirit. Talk about the importance of being on time, working with a good attitude at even the most simple or menial tasks, being cheerful and helpful to customers (even babysitters have customers—the kids they are taking care of and their parents.)

Even if your children are not ready to work outside the home, you can apply these same principles to doing chores around the house, doing homework, keeping their rooms neat and tidy, etc.

Our character is not something we can put on and off like a piece of clothing. Our character is what slips out of us as we go about our day-to-day tasks. If we are hard-working, this will show in all that we do. If we are sloppy, that also will leak out in how we perform different tasks.

Discuss the fact that every job has aspects that we find pleasant and aspects that we don't enjoy. It is the way we handle what we don't like that really shows who we are inside. Are we cheerful or do we complain? Do we work at everything with all our heart or are there some things we slack off on?

PLANS, COMMiTMENTS OR FOLLOW UP

Share with each other ways that this devotional has challenged and encouraged you. Ask each person one way they want to change to become more like Daniel in the passage you read together earlier. Pray together about those changes. During the week that follows encourage each other daily to have the hard-working, no compromising character that Daniel had.

SCRipTURe MeMeRY eR ADDiTienal STUDY

Proverbs 6:6–8
Colossians 3:23–24

Live a 'Two-Mile' Lifestyle

Matthew 5:38–42

OBJECTIVE

The preteen and teen years can be some of the most challenging as our children go through so many changes. Hormonal changes get added to the mixture of going to new schools, learning to change classes, getting accustomed to having many teachers, friendship issues, etc. All these things and more can add up to our children becoming moody, self-centered and insecure. One way to battle all these character attributes is to help them focus on others and on being the kind of person who goes "the second mile." This devotional is designed to help foster this heart in our family.

ACTIVITY

During the day or two leading up to the devotional, Mom and Dad should practice great two-mile behavior. In every situation where one person asks the other to do something, the response should be something like "Of course, Honey, what else can I do for you?" Or, "Is there anything else that you need?" Go out of your way to exaggerate the responses and see if the kids start to notice. They may say something, or they may just shake their heads (or roll their eyes).

At the beginning of the devotional, ask if anyone has noticed anything different the last day or two. (Maybe your house is different than ours, and Mom and Dad don't need to practice—if so we commend you and hope you keep up the great example for your children!)

APPLICATION

Read Matthew 5:38–42, really focusing on verse 41. Discuss what it means to go the second mile. Explain the background on this statement: Israel was under the control of the Romans during this time. A Roman soldier could make an Israelite carry his burden for a mile, but at the end of the mile, the person did not have to carry the burden any more. You can just imagine that person saying, "I carried it for a mile, and that's it. No more!"

Jesus says someone might force you to go one mile with them, but that you should be willing then to go the second mile. How does it make you feel when someone goes out of their way for you? How does it make you feel to go out of your way for others? So often we can be selfish and grudgingly do something we are asked to do by a friend, parent, teacher or child. When you respond that way, how does it make you feel?

Parents, share how your heart changed over the time you started practicing going the second mile for each other. It may have started out as a "lesson" for the kids, but what did it make you realize about yourselves? Was it a part of your lifestyle with each other? What did it make you realize about your family? How have you decided to be different?

Share these things with your children. It will help them realize that change is good and possible at all stages of life and that they are not the only ones who need to make changes in the home. Our changes can be powerful statements of God's power for our children.

Discuss the positive responses that come from being a second-mile kind of person. How can your children apply this principle at school in their classes? How about with their friends? How can everyone apply this principle at home? Parents, share how you plan to become a two-mile employee or employer.

PLans, CoMMitMents oR FoLLoW UP

Hand-make or print out a sign on the computer that simply says "Two-Mile Lifestyle" and post it as a reminder on the door that everyone uses to leave the house every day. Have fun trying to out-do each other in going the extra mile at home. Discuss how it's going over dinner, and help each other think of ways to apply this to various areas of our lives.

For example, how would someone mow the lawn if they were living a two-mile lifestyle? (Trimming and sweeping up instead of simply mowing and putting everything away.) How would you do the dishes? (Cleaning the sink and counter tops as well.) Make this a fun adventure for the whole family instead of a heavy-handed devotional to "make everyone change."

SCRIPtURe MeMoRY oR ADDitional StUDY

Philippians 2:5–8
Philippians 2:14–16

Don't Pop Under Peer Pressure

Galatians 1:10

Objective

Our children face pressure every day to live and act like the world. They face pressure from their friends at school (and sometimes from those at church as well) to dress, talk, watch things and act in ways to fit in with the world. This devotional gives your family a great opportunity to discuss the pressure they face and come up with ways to deal with everything without giving in.

Activity

Give everyone in the family a balloon and have them blow it up as big as possible and tie the end. Then one by one have each person squeeze their balloon until it pops. Discuss what made the balloons pop and how much pressure each person had to use to make their balloon pop. Some balloons probably popped immediately, while others kept jiggling and moving from end to end before they caved in.

APPLiCaTion

Read Galatians 1:10. Discuss what it means to be a people-pleaser. How can wanting to please men keep us from serving God? In what ways can we be tempted to want the approval of our friends, rather than desiring the approval of God?

Children aren't the only ones that face peer pressure. Parents, share how pressure from coworkers can sometimes tempt you to do or say things that God would not approve of. Or share times from growing up when you remember giving in to your friends and doing something that went against your conscience.

Discuss situations your children are facing that might be tempting for them. Some things that our kids have faced include making fun of and being disrespectful of teachers at school, listening to jokes that are lewd, dressing immodestly, "swearing" to fit in with friends from school, lying or cheating on school work so that people will accept them, or gossiping about other classmates or kids at church.

Ask your children if they have faced any of these things or others. Ask how they have handled the temptations. It is important to listen and be empathetic as they share about the temptations they have faced. We have come to realize just how difficult it is for our preteens and young teens to keep facing some of these challenges day in and day out. The pressure can be relentless for them, seeming to never end.

Thank your children for being open with you about the challenges they are facing, and encourage them to stay open about them. If a balloon never gets air, it can't pop. In the same way, the more open we are about our temptations and things that are challenging for us to face, the less likely we will be to fill up and pop under the pressure of giving in to our friends.

Another strategy you can use to help your children stay strong in the face of peer pressure is to talk through each temptation specifically. Help them think through the consequences of giving in to the temptations to gossip or cheat or swear or look at pornographic photos in magazines or on the Internet. Something may seem really little to them, but if we can help paint the bigger picture, they might be motivated to turn away instead of being drawn toward sin.

PLANS, COMMITMENTS OR FOLLOW UP

Pray together at the end of the devotional for everyone to want to please God rather than men. Pin up two balloons somewhere for everyone to see during the next week. Blow up one balloon really big and just hang the other one empty beside it as a reminder for everyone to avoid giving in to peer pressure. Ask your children periodically how things are going in the different areas they shared about.

SCRIPTURE MEMORY OR ADDITIONAL STUDY

Matthew 26:69–75

WHAT DO YOU BELIEVE?

Matthew 16:13–20

OBJECTIVE

The preteen and young teen years are times of great growth and provide a great opportunity for our kids to explore their beliefs. Often this is a scary time for parents, who want their children to accept all they have been taught and move on quickly to a life totally devoted to God. It is important that our children feel the freedom to express questions about their faith and even to express doubts about what they have read and been taught. It is a healthy process and one we read about even with the disciples that followed Jesus.

This devotional helps our kids to think about what they believe and to realize that Jesus really cares what they think. Using a family devotional to bring up this topic can reassure our children that we understand their need to develop their own faith and may open the door some great honest discussions down the road.

ACTIVITY

Start this devotional playing a game of charades or a game of "Who am I?" To play "Who am I?" pick several famous people or people that your family is close to and list three to four things about them that are unique. Read the list out loud and have everyone guess who the person is.

APPLicatiΘn

After playing the game, read Matthew 16:13–20 together. Perhaps in the game you played there was some confusion about who the character or person was that you were trying to act out or guess. There was also some confusion about who Jesus was. People were guessing all kinds of things about him.

Even today people have many opinions and ideas about who Jesus is.

Jesus already knew what people were saying about him. In asking the disciples, what he really wanted to know was who his followers said he was. We each have to answer that same question in our own lives: who do we believe Jesus is? It is a great benefit to grow up going to church as a family, reading the Bible together and having friendships with other families that believe the same things you believe. But each person has to come to their own, individual faith.

People were surrounding Jesus and watching him all the time. They saw the miracles he was performing, they saw how he spoke to people, how he treated people from all different walks of life. The apostles saw everything as well. When Peter claimed that Jesus was the Son of God, Jesus praised him and explained that God had shown him who Jesus really was.

How did God show Peter who Jesus was? How do you think that Peter came to believe Jesus was the Son of God? How do you think that Peter grew in his faith? How can we grow in our faith? How can each of us overcome all the confusion in the world about Jesus?

Do you think the apostles ever had doubts about who Jesus was? (Refer to Matthew 28:17 and John 20:24–31—read them together if you have time). Yes, the disciples had doubts and fears, just like we do today. Jesus helped them overcome their doubts, and he will also help us overcome any doubts or fears we have in developing a strong faith in who he is.

Ask your children if they ever doubt that what they have learned growing up is true? Assure them that it is okay to have doubts. Part of growing and developing a strong faith is having questions and getting those questions answered. If they do have questions, answer any simple things in the time you have together, or suggest that you spend more time later talking, studying and finding answers. (Make sure you initiate time to study together soon!)

Plans, Commitments or Follow Up

Pray together for everyone in the family to develop their own strong faith in Jesus. You might want to read *More Than a Carpenter* by Josh McDowell or *Mere Christianity* by C. S. Lewis. You could read together as a family or suggest that your children read one of them on their own. (You know the maturity level of your children and whether they would profit from reading books like these.) Let your children know that you are always interested in what they are thinking and learning and want to discuss any questions they may have.

Keep the doors open for them to come and ask questions and treat their questions with faith and respect, knowing that God will help you guide them on their journey to having a strong faith in God and his word.

Scripture Memory or Additional Study

John 4:42

43

BE a GooD SPORT

Philippians 2:3–4

OBJECTIVE

In our competitive culture, it is important to teach our children to be good sports and to consider others before themselves whether they win or lose some type of game. This devotional focuses on having a lot of fun together playing your family's favorite games and using the time to talk together about this important concept.

ACTIVITY AND APPLICATION

This devotional is a little different because your application may actually start the fun family activities for the evening.

Pick a game to play for the evening that everyone in your family enjoys. Honestly, for our family it can be a challenge to choose a game that everyone gets excited about playing. We are all competitive by nature and often want to play the game that we are best at. So this devotional is really good for us.

Start off by reading Philippians 2:3–4 and talk about what it means to consider others "better" (or before) yourself when you're playing a game. Is it wrong to want to win? No, in 1 Corinthians 9:24 Paul acknowledges that in a race all the runners run to win the prize. It is good to do the best you can do at any activity.

The problem comes when winning is the only thing that matters. Look at the different elements of Philippians 2:3–4. Discuss what it means to look not only to your own interests but also to the interests of others. (For example, encouraging other players when they make a good play or when they get a good roll of the dice.) Being a good sport means that while you want to be the winner, you also want to recognize others for doing a good job and to be glad for their opportunities to shine.

Another aspect of being a good sport in team events is encouraging other members of the team to do their best and recognizing their efforts along with your own. How does being humble show in being a good sport? If you battle with being conceited, how does that keep you from being a good sport?

What is selfish ambition? How does selfish ambition keep you from being a good sport? Is it good sportsmanship to sulk when you are losing or have lost a game? Why not? What is a better way to react and behave? How can you express disappointment and still be a good sport?

Spend the evening or afternoon playing games, and help each other put these lessons into practice as you play. Encourage good sportsmanship and help anyone whose behavior needs a little correction. Make it a fun family time that builds great memories. Also, remember that practice makes perfect, so schedule game nights often! Let the loser of the game pick the game the family will play the next time.

Plans, Commitments or Follow Up

Purchase or make enough 1st place ribbons for everyone in your family to have one. At the end of your games, hold a ribbon ceremony, honoring everyone for becoming a number one good sportsman. While none of us can be winners at everything we try, we can all be winners in having the character of being humble and considering others before ourselves. Post the ribbons someplace where everyone can be reminded to show good sportsmanship during the week.

Scripture Memory or Additional Study

John 13:34–35

44

A GENTLE ANSWER IS BEST

Proverbs 15:1

OBJECTIVE

Sibling relationships can be some of the best and also some of the most challenging in our lives. Teaching our children to love one another, to be respectful and to be patient with each other is a constant lesson we need to be focused on as parents. This devotional is aimed at helping our kids learn the best ways to speak with one another. If you only have one child, then you can make application to relationships with friends.

ACTIVITY

Start this devotional with a discussion about relationships. Have each person tell what they love most about their best friend and explain what makes their friendship so good. Ask if friends ever have differences of opinion or disagreements. Ask if they ever hurt each other's feelings. What do they do in those situations? How do they resolve the conflict?

The Bible says that our sinfulness causes us to fight and quarrel (see James 1:19). We do not treat others the way we would like to be treated. Yet we expect them to be nice to us, even when we have been ugly to them. Is that fair? Read Proverbs 15:1 together. Discuss the following questions.

1. When you are angry, which helps you to calm down and be able to express your feelings in an un-hurtful way—a patient reaction or an angry response from someone? Why?

2. Do you appreciate it when people are patient even when you have not been very nice to them? How does that help you to change your attitude?

Sometimes people have bad days, or maybe they are just feeling bad about something. We all need a little extra love at those times. An ungodly reaction to someone's careless words is like pouring gas on a fire. Things can get ugly really fast. And then people end up really hurting each other. (Note: Make sure your children realize that it is wrong to start an argument or provoke a sibling. After this is established, then explore the importance of godly reactions to an ugly comment.)

Application

A brother or a sister is a precious gift from God. He wants us to cherish and protect that relationship. Some people never learn how to love their siblings. Sometimes they get angry over something, even something unimportant, and don't speak to each other for years. That is really sad.

We, your parents, don't ever want that to happen to you. You would damage or possibly lose a gift that God intended as a special life-long relationship. Learning how to love each other even when we are sometimes unlovable is so important. When you do that you are imitating Jesus, who loved us and died for us when we weren't lovable.

In your lives there will be many times when you will have to decide how you are going to react to someone who says or does something you don't like. Can you think of an example this week of someone saying something to you in the family or at church or school that was upsetting to you? How did you respond?

It is important to learn how to respond in a godly way. This will help you for the rest of your life—in your relationships with friends, bosses, coworkers and people in general.

God has given us families to nurture very special relationships and to learn these important lessons. A warm, loving family is wonderful indeed (whether it has one or two parents or whether there are ten children or just one). In fact, God calls the church a family and he tells us how to treat each other in that special family.

Plans, Commitments or Follow Up

What could we do on a daily basis to learn to love our siblings more? (It starts with our hearts. We need to be sure we think more about the things we love about our brothers or sisters than their faults. We could start actively treating each other the way we would like to be treated.) Maybe we could start right now...let's go around the circle and let each person say one thing they love about Susan. Then we can all say one thing we appreciate most about Jason...etc.

Close with a prayer asking God to bless the family and to help us watch over our hearts so we will love and not hurt the people he loves and we love.

Scripture Memory or Additional Study

Galatians 5:22–23

Additional Suggestions

You should adapt and adjust this in view of the ages of your children and their particular needs. Sometimes you must look beyond appearances (pray for wisdom!) to get at the real issues that cause conflict. For example, older kids may complain about the provocative behavior of younger brothers and sisters. Yet, sometimes the younger ones do not feel considered and loved by the older ones, who use their physical strength and more advanced intellect to put down and humiliate the younger ones. It becomes a cycle of hurting each other and both are to blame (although we should expect more mature behavior from a fifteen-year-old than a ten-year-old).

Also, as you discuss different issues, you may want to address some things in the devotional, and then later follow up with the kids individually if you feel it would be humiliating to talk to them about something in their character in front of the others. Humiliation will cause a child to close up right away, and communication stops.

DiSReSPeCT iS DaNGeRoUS

Numbers 12

(This devotional is revisited from the first volume of *As for Me and My House*, with a few changes that will help it apply to your preteens and young teens. Although this is a heavier topic than some, learning to be respectful is a life lesson that will help our children shine in all that they do.)

OBJeCtiVe

Our children are growing up in a world in which respect is a dying trait. Watching the television shows that are on Disney Channel and other "kid friendly" channels have convinced us that we must counteract things our children are being taught are normal. We must teach them that although movies, books or friends might be disrespectful, God does not tolerate it! Numbers 12 is a powerful and frightening example of God's attitude toward criticizing his authority.

ACtiViTY

Watch one of your child's favorite television shows together. Almost any show you choose will depict the kids being disrespectful of the adults in their lives. Television is creating the illusion that kids know best and that parents, teachers and others in authority really need a lot of help.

APPLication

Before you read the scripture, discuss with your children what it means to be respectful. Ask them to give you examples of respect. After this, ask them what it means to be disrespectful. Ask them to give you specific examples of disrespect. Talk with them about tone of voice, attitude, body language, etc. and how each of these things can show respect or disrespect. Perhaps give specific examples and act them out showing both respect and disrespect. (Rolling your eyes, heavy sighs, sarcasm, heavy steps, repeat the offenses of a parent, teacher, etc.) Discuss the show you watched together and ask for examples of both respect and disrespect. Even "dissing" friends can be disrespectful (if you don't know what that means, ask your kids for an explanation—they'll know!).

Read Numbers 12. It is a short chapter and very specific. If time doesn't permit reading the whole chapter, then read only verses 1–3 and 9–12. Tell the rest of the story briefly in your own words.

After reading, go back to the discussion you had previously with your children and apply this story of Miriam being disrespectful of Moses, her leader, and of God. Ask them how God feels about being disrespectful of his leadership. Ask what forms of leadership God puts in their lives: parents, teachers, policemen, other adults, church leaders, etc. How does God feel when we criticize his authority?

Why is disrespect so bad? What does it do to relationships? How does it hurt?

Does criticism ever help solve problems? Does being disrespectful ever solve problems? Help your children understand that God hates disrespect and that he will not tolerate it in our lives. Ask each child if they can see ways that they personally show disrespect at times.

Parents, we need to model respect just like every other character trait we expect from our children. Moms, have you been respectful toward your husband? How do you speak to and about him? Our kids hear everything. We need to be honest about how we need to change as well and apologize to everyone if we haven't been showing respect at home.

About the story of Miriam in Numbers: let the children know that a story like this in the Old Testament is to help us learn a lesson. It does not mean that God will strike us with a disease if we are disrespectful. But it does mean that God takes disrespect very seriously and will not bless us in the ways he would like to if we persist in disrespect.

Plans, Commitments or Follow up

End this devotional with a prayer and have each person pray specifically about being respectful of each other at all times. At dinner during the week discuss what everyone learned from Numbers 12. Use this time to evaluate how each child (and parent) is doing in showing respect to authority. Give lots of praise for every improvement and encourage change where it is needed. Let your children know that you believe this is something they can change and that it is a life lesson they need to learn.

Scripture Memory or Additional Study

1 Peter 2:17

46

Rejoice and Laugh Together

Psalm 126:1–3, Genesis 21:6–7

Objective

Life can be hard sometimes, and we all face difficult situations and disappointments.

Laughter can be one of the best tools we use to help us through difficult times. It also makes the good times even better. Whatever the general atmosphere is at your home, this devotional will help remind everyone that God is a good and powerful God who wants us to enjoy the life he has given us.

Activity

Watch a funny television show or movie together. Parents, you may be able to find an old Laurel and Hardy video (or other slapstick comedy) and introduce your kids to humor that your parents introduced to you! Our family loves to watch *America's Funniest Home Videos*. Or get a book of jokes from the library and take turns telling the jokes.

APPLication

Hopefully, whatever activity you chose made your family laugh long and hard. Read Psalm 126:1–2 together. The Israelites had been through a difficult time of captivity, and when they came back to Zion, they just couldn't stop laughing! Their mouths were filled with laughter. What picture does that bring up in your mind? They were so happy that they just couldn't stop the flow of laughter.

Sarah experienced similar feelings when God enabled her to enjoy the privilege of having a child at a very old age! Look at Genesis 21:6–7. She expected that everyone who knew her or heard about her having a child was going to laugh right along with her! Babies and children bring a lot of joy to our lives, especially if we had to wait for them like Sarah did!

Discuss how amazing it is that God created us with the capacity for laughter. Why would he have given us this ability?

Tell your children some of the joyful, funny things you remember about them as babies. Our children can never get enough of hearing about themselves, and we spend a lot of time laughing about their antics. There is a saying that laughter is the best medicine. There is a lot of truth in that. God really wants us to enjoy our lives and he wants us to laugh and have fun together.

Ask your family to recall some of the best memories they have of your times together. Chances are, those memories will revolve around things that make everyone smile and laugh together.

Plans, Commitments or Follow up

Keep a book of jokes in the house to read after dinner. Or have a joke of the day contest. It is too easy to get caught up in the problems of life and forget to relax and laugh together. Keeping the atmosphere light-hearted at home will make it the haven God wants for us to have.

Scripture Memory or Additional Study

Philippians 4:4, Proverbs 17:22

47

WHO WILL YOU Date?

2 Corinthians 6:14–18

OBJECTIVE

Dating can be an emotionally charged topic in many households. Every parent has opinions about when to allow their children to date, how they can date and how serious things should get at any given age. We hope this devotional will help your family discuss some principles that will make dating a joy in your family and not a battleground. You may think your preteen is too young to tackle this topic, but we hear about kids at school who start pairing up in the third and fourth grade.

ACTIVITY

Get a picture of a yoke (from a book or the Internet) to show your kids, and describe how animals are joined at the head or neck for working together. If two animals of different weights and sizes (say an ox and a donkey) are yoked together, the bigger animal will pull the smaller one along by the neck, choking it and causing a lot of pain.

To illustrate this, take two belts and put one around Mom or Dad's neck and the other around one of your kid's necks. Notch the belts so they are loose. Use tape (masking or duct tape would work well) to join the ends together between the two people. Let them take turns trying to get the other person to go their way. Explain that when two animals of similar size and weight are yoked, they more easily work together to pull or plow smoothly, helping each other and getting a lot of work accomplished.

Application

Read 2 Corinthians 6:14–18. Ask how this passage applies to dating. What would happen if you chose to date someone who had different values and beliefs than you do? What are some different ideas about dating that you and a person who doesn't share your faith could have about dating? Discuss what could happen if you date someone that is stronger in his/her opinions than you are. How could that pull you away from God? How might having different convictions about dating practices cause problems in the relationship?

This is not the only passage that God uses to direct our path in the topic of dating and marriage. In the Old Testament, God tells the Israelites in Deuteronomy 7:3–4 not to give their sons and daughters in marriage to the foreigners around them, as that would make them turn from God. In Judges 14 and 16, Sampson chooses to marry women from the surrounding communities two different times, both of which proved disastrous. Of course, we follow the New Testament nowadays, but these examples from the Old Testament help us to know the principles that are on God's heart.

Discuss the idea that while your children are obviously too young for marriage, someday the person they choose to marry will be a person that they have dated. What are some important things to consider in dating? How do people in our world decide who to date? What have your children seen at school or in the television shows they watch? What role should friendship play in dating?

End your devotional with a prayer that each child will have a great time dating as they get older and that they will eventually marry someone who loves God with all their heart and will help your child stay close to God always.

Plans, Commitments or Follow Up

Find time during the next week to speak individually with

your children about the devotional. Ask how they felt about it and how it helped them. If they say they haven't really thought about it much since, give them space and realize you planted seeds that will take root at the right time.

SCRIPTURE MEMORY OR ADDITIONAL STUDY

Jeremiah 29:11

GOD'S TREASURE

Deuteronomy 7:6, Matthew 6:26

OBJECTIVE

The Israelites were the apple of God's eye, as we are today. God loves us deeply and longs to be close to us and to take care of us. This devotional will help your family focus on God's love for us.

ACTIVITY

Plan a treasure hunt for the family. Make up clues and hide something of great value to your family (maybe a box of everyone's favorite treats to share at the end of the devotional). You can make a treasure map or you could hand out one clue to start that leads everyone to the second and the third and so on, until they find the treasure.

APPLICATION

Once the treasure has been found, have everyone sit together and talk about the treasure hunt. Was it fun? Did anyone guess what the treasure might be before it was found? Were the clues easy or hard? Why is it fun to go on a treasure hunt? Why is it fun to find treasure?

How do you know what someone treasures? Read what

Deuteronomy 7:6 says. Describe how God felt about the Israelites. What does it mean that they were God's treasured possession? What do you have that you treasure? How do you treat the things that you treasure? How does God treat us?

While we are not living by the laws of the Old Testament, learning about how God felt about his people is important for us today as well. In Matthew 6:26 the writer reminds us that God takes care of the birds, and we are much more valuable than they are. God doesn't want us to worry; he wants us to trust him. We can trust God when we understand how much he loves us and how he has our best interest at heart all the time.

How does it make you feel to know that God loves you and that you are his treasured possession? How does it inspire you to respond to God's commands, knowing that he wrote them for our good, to take care of us?

Plans, Commitments or Follow Up

Post the clues or the treasure map on the refrigerator during the week to remind everyone that they are God's treasure. Pray together daily, thanking God for his love and for all the blessings he gives us because he loves us so much.

Scripture Memory or Additional Study

Psalm 17:8
Psalm 100:3

49

OVERFLOWING WITH THANKFULNESS

Colossians 2:7b, 1 Thessalonians 5:18

OBJECTIVE

The more thankful we are in our lives, the happier and more contented we will be. If we focus on what we don't have or can't do, then we often find ourselves complaining or feeling sorry for ourselves. This devotional helps us to think of all the ways God blesses our lives every day and just how much we have to be grateful for.

ACTIVITY

Start off by asking one of the kids to hold a glass. Get a pitcher that is full of water, and start pouring it into the glass. Talk about how the Bible tells us to overflow with thankfulness. Keep pouring the water as you talk until it flows over the top of the glass, surprising the "holder."

Then ask is this how thankful we are, or this: hand another glass to someone else to hold, and just pour about a fourth of a glass of water. It is hard for a glass to overflow when it has so little water in it. And so it is with us if we have so little thankfulness in lives.

Spend time singing together to help everyone focus on how good God is to us. Songs like, "Thank you Lord," "Amazing Grace," and "His Love Endures Forever" are great songs to set the stage for this devotional time. You could also ask each of your children to lead their favorite song.

APPLicatiən

Read Colossians 2:7b. What does it mean to be overflowing? What are some things that overflow? (Washing machines, popcorn makers, rivers...) When something is overflowing, can you hide it? When something overflows, how does it affect things around it? God tells us here to be overflowing with thankfulness. How can we tell if someone is overflowing with thankfulness? What is their speech like? How does it affect their mood? How does it affect how they treat people around them?

What is the opposite of being thankful? (Complaining, moaning, being bitter.) How does a lack of being thankful affect our speech and our mood?

Now look at 1 Thessalonians 5:18. God tells us here to be thankful in all circumstances. Discuss what that really means. Discuss how that can be difficult to do at times and think of reasons why it can be difficult. Why does God want us to be thankful in all circumstances?

Talk about things that can be challenging to overcome. Maybe your children don't like school or certain subjects at school. How can they learn to be thankful? Most girls (and some boys) have a bad hair day at least once in a while. How does that affect their speech and attitude? How can we learn to be thankful in those times? Often times it is the "little" things that can throw us off course and make us complain rather than be thankful.

Make a list together of all the things you have to be grateful for as a family. Keep going around the room until you have a pretty hefty list. Then read the list out loud. End the devotional with a prayer to thank God for all the many ways he has blessed your family.

Plans, cəmmitments ər Fəllow up

Post your family's list on the refrigerator or a bulletin board so everyone can see it during the week. Make it a goal for every person to add one new thing to the list that they are thankful for every day. Let everyone know that the goal is for the page(s) to be overflowing! Watch how this exercise changes your family's focus and how it changes individual attitudes during the week. Encourage the growth you witness in each person's life.

SCRIPTURE MEMORY OR ADDITIONAL STUDY

Psalm 136:1

50

LIVING GOD'S WAY

Joshua 1:8, 1 John 5:3

OBJECTIVE

In this devotional we will look at the commands that God gave to the children of Israel as they entered the promised land. He gave them these commands because he loved them and knew what would make them successful and happy. Sometimes we and our kids might think that God's commands keep us from having a good time or are a burden to keep. This devotional helps our families to understand that God only wants what is best for us and that is why he tells us how to live.

ACTIVITY

Choose a board game like *Monopoly* or *Sorry* for the family to play. Tell the kids that this time you are going to play it a little differently. Forget about the rules that you usually use to play the game. Each person can make up their own rules as they go along. Make a big deal about how much fun this will be not to have to worry about the rules of the game—how freeing it will be.

Then say quickly something like, "I am the oldest person here, and the oldest person gets to go first. So I go first." Then make up another rule during your turn that is totally in your favor.

Encourage your spouse and/or children to jump in with their rules. "If you are the green piece, you can automatically move your piece to the finish. You don't even have to roll the dice." You get the idea. After just a few minutes, it will become obvious that this is not going to work out.

Stop the game and say, "What is the problem here?" Chaos will be reigning until you rein it in.

APPLICation

Read Joshua 1:8 and explain that this is what God is saying to the Israelites as they are entering the land he had promised them.

Why did God tell the Israelites how to live? Did he just want to boss them around and make a bunch of rules to keep them from having fun? (No, he wanted them to be happy and successful in life.) Why would he know what would make them happy and successful? (He made them and he loved them, and he knew what was best for them.)

To make the point, use this example: ask the kids to put themselves in the place of a train who has to stay on the tracks all the time. As it passes the beautiful fields of grass, it looks longingly upon them and wishes it could jump off the tracks and go out into the fields. It feels confined by just having to go on the tracks.

What would happen if it did jump off the tracks and head for the fields? (It would immediately bog down and stop.) Why would it stop? (It was made to run on tracks.) What is it free to do if it does run on the tracks? (It is free to race and run and go many places.) What lesson do you think the train would learn by trying to run in the field? How does this example apply to our discussion about God having certain rules for us and certain ways for us to live? What happens to our lives if we try to make up our own rules and do our own thing?

Read 1 John 5:3. What is one way we show God that we love him? What does "burdensome" mean? Why are God's commands not burdensome?

Like the train on the tracks, God longs for us to do all we were made to do. As we seek to love him and to obey him, he will help us to live lives that are successful and happy.

Plans, Commitments or Follow Up

Go ahead and play the game with the rules. Discuss how much more fun it is when we all know the rules of play and abide by them. We are more encouraging to each other and we have a peace and calm that was missing when we were all making up our own rules.

Scripture Memory or Additional Study

Psalm 119:32

CONTRiBUTORS OF DeVOTiONALS AND iDeAS

Thank you to all who offered whole devotionals and ideas that fueled several of the devotionals written for the book. The contributors' names are listed below.

Ed Anton, Hampton Roads, Virginia
Frederic and Mary Bea Bouchet, Mannassas, Virginia
Beverly Janka, Leesburg, Virginia
Chris & LaLisa Jones, Fredericksburg, Virginia
Sheila Jones, Nashville, Tennessee
Brett Kreider, Herndon, Virginia
Mike and Faith Levy, Herndon, Virginia
Erik and Vida Li Sik, Johannesburg, South Africa
Janet Marks, Coppell, Texas
Tony Millet, Hampton Roads, Virginia
Kinny Pesquera, Potomac Falls, Maryland
Cathy Rosenquist, Herndon, Virginia

aterial for mor Devotionals

Bible Stories for Your Children

To further help you develop your children's love for God's word, we are providing two lists of basic Bible stories (Old Testament and New Testament) and one list of scriptures with topics to teach at home. You can read them as part of daily quiet times with your children, or you can imitate the format used for the family devotionals to develop your own devotionals from these stories. Or you could do both! We hope this helps you build a strong, spiritual family that loves the word of God.

Old Testament Stories

1. Creation (Genesis 1)
2. Adam and Eve (Genesis 2-3)
3. Cain and Abel (Genesis 4)
4. Noah and the Ark (Genesis 6-8)
5. The Tower of Babel (Genesis 11)
6. Sodom and Gomorrah (Genesis 18:16-19:29)
7. Abraham Sacrifices Isaac (Genesis 22)
8. Joseph and His Coat of Many Colors (Genesis 37:1-11)
9. Joseph in Jail and His Vision (Genesis 40-41)
10. Moses' Birth (Exodus 2)
11. Moses and the Burning Bush (Exodus 3)
12. Moses and the Plagues (Exodus 7-11)
13. Moses Parts the Red Sea (Exodus 13:17-14:31)
14. Manna from Heaven (Exodus 16)
15. The Golden Calf (Exodus 32)
16. The Rewards for Obedience (Leviticus 26)
17. Miriam and Aaron Oppose Moses (Numbers 12)
18. The Twelve Spies Sent into Canaan (Numbers 13; Deuteronomy 1:19-46)
19. The Bronze Snake (Numbers 21:4-9)
20. Balaam's Donkey (Numbers 22:21-41)
21. Be Strong and Courageous (Joshua 1)
22. Joshua and the Battle of Jericho (Joshua 5:13-6:27)

23. Achan's Sin (Joshua 7)
24. Sun Stands Still (Joshua 10:1-15)
25. Ehud and Eglon (Judges 3:12-30)
26. Deborah (Judges 4)
27. Gideon (Judges 6-7)
28. Samson (Judges 13-16)
29. Ruth and Naomi (Ruth)
30. David and Goliath (1 Samuel 17)
31. Jonathan and David (1 Samuel 18-20)
32. Abigail (1 Samuel 25)
33. David's Mighty Men (2 Samuel 23:8-39;
    1 Chronicles 11:10-47)
34. Solomon and the Women with the Baby (1 Kings 3:16-28)
35. Elijah on Mount Carmel (1 Kings 18:16-46)
36. Elijah Carried up to Heaven (2 Kings 2)
37. Naaman (2 Kings 5)
38. Jezebel Eaten by Dogs (2 Kings 9:30-37)
39. Hezekiah (2 Kings 18-20)
40. Josiah (2 Kings 22-23)
41. Solomon and the Queen of Sheba (2 Chronicles 9)
42. Esther
43. Job (1–2:10; 30–42)
44. Shadrach, Meshach and Abednego (Daniel 3)
45. Daniel and the Lions' Den (Daniel 6)
46. Jonah and the Fish (Jonah 1-4)

New Testament Stories

1. The Birth of Jesus (Luke 1)
2. The Birth of John the Baptist (Luke 1)
3. Gabriel's Appearance to Mary (Luke 1:26-38)
4. Jesus As a Boy in the Temple (Luke 2:41-52)
5. Jesus Heals a Leper (Mark 1:40-45; Luke 5:12-16)
6. The Temptation of Jesus (Matthew 4:1-11)
7. The Crucifixion (Matthew 26-28)
8. The Samaritan Woman at the Well (John 4)
9. The Prodigal Son (Luke 15:11-32)
10. The Parable of the Sower (Matthew 13:1-23)
11. The Feeding the Five Thousand (Matthew 14:13-21;
    Mark 6:30-44)
12. The Rich Young Man (Matthew 19:16-30)

13. The Parable of the Two Sons (Matthew 21:28-32)
14. The Parable of the Wedding Banquet (Matthew 22:1-14)
15. The Parable of the Talents (Matthew 25:14-30)
16. Jesus Walking on the Water (Matthew 14:22-36; Mark 6:45-56)
17. Widow's Offering (Mark 12:41-44; Luke 21:1-4)
18. The Sheep and Goats (Matthew 25:31-46)
19. Driving Demons into the Pigs (Mark 5:1-20)
20. Healing the Paralytic (Mark 2)
21. Good Samaritan (Luke 10:25-37)
22. The Persistent Widow (Luke 18:1-8)
23. The Pharisee and Tax Collector (Luke 18:9-14)
24. The Good Shepherd (John 10:1-21)
25. Lazarus (John 11:1-44)
26. Pentecost (Acts 2)
27. Saul on the Road to Damascus (Acts 9:1-19)
28. Saul in a Basket over the Wall (Acts 9:19b-31)
29. Ethiopian Eunuch (Acts 8:26-40)
30. Peter's Miraculous Escape (Acts 12:1-19)
31. Lydia (Acts 16:11-15)
32. Jailer (Acts 16:16-40)
33. Paul's Shipwreck (Acts 27:1-28:10)

ADDitional IDeas

Matthew 5-7
Each heading in these three chapters makes a great quiet time. They also provide great discussion topics for family dinners. Your family could spend a month going through these chapters together.

John 5:1-15
This passage is great for talking about making excuses.

2 Corinthians 12:1-10
God works though our weaknesses.

Ephesians 3:20-21
Use this passage to meditate on God's amazing power.

Philippians 2:12-18
Shine, don't complain.

Philippians 3:12-14
 Don't let mistakes or victories stop you from growing.

1 Timothy 4:12-16
 You can set a great example!

Hebrews 11
 God's Hall of Faith will help build your child's faith.

Hebrews 12:1-13
 Everyone gets disciplined sometime!

James 1:19-25
 Don't just listen—you must do what God says.